C-463 CAREER EXAMINATION SERIES

This is your
PASSBOOK for...

Maintenance Man (Worker)

Test Preparation Study Guide
Questions & Answers

COPYRIGHT NOTICE

This book is SOLELY intended for, is sold ONLY to, and its use is RESTRICTED to individual, bona fide applicants or candidates who qualify by virtue of having seriously filed applications for appropriate license, certificate, professional and/or promotional advancement, higher school matriculation, scholarship, or other legitimate requirements of education and/or governmental authorities.

This book is NOT intended for use, class instruction, tutoring, training, duplication, copying, reprinting, excerption, or adaptation, etc., by:

1) Other publishers
2) Proprietors and/or Instructors of "Coaching" and/or Preparatory Courses
3) Personnel and/or Training Divisions of commercial, industrial, and governmental organizations
4) Schools, colleges, or universities and/or their departments and staffs, including teachers and other personnel
5) Testing Agencies or Bureaus
6) Study groups which seek by the purchase of a single volume to copy and/or duplicate and/or adapt this material for use by the group as a whole without having purchased individual volumes for each of the members of the group
7) Et al.

Such persons would be in violation of appropriate Federal and State statutes.

PROVISION OF LICENSING AGREEMENTS – Recognized educational, commercial, industrial, and governmental institutions and organizations, and others legitimately engaged in educational pursuits, including training, testing, and measurement activities, may address request for a licensing agreement to the copyright owners, who will determine whether, and under what conditions, including fees and charges, the materials in this book may be used them. In other words, a licensing facility exists for the legitimate use of the material in this book on other than an individual basis. However, it is asseverated and affirmed here that the material in this book CANNOT be used without the receipt of the express permission of such a licensing agreement from the Publishers. Inquiries re licensing should be addressed to the company, attention rights and permissions department.

All rights reserved, including the right of reproduction in whole or in part, in any form or by any means, electronic or mechanical, including photocopying, recording, or by any information storage and retrieval system, without permission in writing from the Publisher.

Copyright © 2024 by
National Learning Corporation

212 Michael Drive, Syosset, NY 11791
(516) 921-8888 • www.passbooks.com
E-mail: info@passbooks.com

PUBLISHED IN THE UNITED STATES OF AMERICA

PASSBOOK® SERIES

THE *PASSBOOK® SERIES* has been created to prepare applicants and candidates for the ultimate academic battlefield – the examination room.

At some time in our lives, each and every one of us may be required to take an examination – for validation, matriculation, admission, qualification, registration, certification, or licensure.

Based on the assumption that every applicant or candidate has met the basic formal educational standards, has taken the required number of courses, and read the necessary texts, the *PASSBOOK® SERIES* furnishes the one special preparation which may assure passing with confidence, instead of failing with insecurity. Examination questions – together with answers – are furnished as the basic vehicle for study so that the mysteries of the examination and its compounding difficulties may be eliminated or diminished by a sure method.

This book is meant to help you pass your examination provided that you qualify and are serious in your objective.

The entire field is reviewed through the huge store of content information which is succinctly presented through a provocative and challenging approach – the question-and-answer method.

A climate of success is established by furnishing the correct answers at the end of each test.

You soon learn to recognize types of questions, forms of questions, and patterns of questioning. You may even begin to anticipate expected outcomes.

You perceive that many questions are repeated or adapted so that you can gain acute insights, which may enable you to score many sure points.

You learn how to confront new questions, or types of questions, and to attack them confidently and work out the correct answers.

You note objectives and emphases, and recognize pitfalls and dangers, so that you may make positive educational adjustments.

Moreover, you are kept fully informed in relation to new concepts, methods, practices, and directions in the field.

You discover that you are actually taking the examination all the time: you are preparing for the examination by "taking" an examination, not by reading extraneous and/or supererogatory textbooks.

In short, this PASSBOOK®, used directedly, should be an important factor in helping you to pass your test.

MAINTENANCE WORKER

DUTIES

Maintenance Workers, under direct supervision, assist in the routine maintenance, operation and repair of public buildings and structures, and the equipment they contain. They conduct visual inspections of building equipment and conditions; maintain, adjust and make minor repairs of building hardware, furniture, shelving and equipment; replace broken window and door glass; repair windows and sashes; make minor repairs to masonry, woodwork, flooring and walls; make minor repairs to building, electrical, plumbing and heating systems; assist in relocating building equipment as directed; keep records; and may operate a motor vehicle in the performance of assigned duties; perform related work.

SCOPE OF THE EXAMINATION

The multiple-choice test may include questions on the basic knowledge of construction techniques and materials; carpentry; plumbing; electrical work; repair and maintenance of mechanical equipment and buildings or facilities; safe working practices and procedures; proper use of tools and equipment, including their design, and, maintenance; and other related areas.

HOW TO TAKE A TEST

I. YOU MUST PASS AN EXAMINATION

A. WHAT EVERY CANDIDATE SHOULD KNOW

Examination applicants often ask us for help in preparing for the written test. What can I study in advance? What kinds of questions will be asked? How will the test be given? How will the papers be graded?

As an applicant for a civil service examination, you may be wondering about some of these things. Our purpose here is to suggest effective methods of advance study and to describe civil service examinations.

Your chances for success on this examination can be increased if you know how to prepare. Those "pre-examination jitters" can be reduced if you know what to expect. You can even experience an adventure in good citizenship if you know why civil service exams are given.

B. WHY ARE CIVIL SERVICE EXAMINATIONS GIVEN?

Civil service examinations are important to you in two ways. As a citizen, you want public jobs filled by employees who know how to do their work. As a job seeker, you want a fair chance to compete for that job on an equal footing with other candidates. The best-known means of accomplishing this two-fold goal is the competitive examination.

Exams are widely publicized throughout the nation. They may be administered for jobs in federal, state, city, municipal, town or village governments or agencies.

Any citizen may apply, with some limitations, such as the age or residence of applicants. Your experience and education may be reviewed to see whether you meet the requirements for the particular examination. When these requirements exist, they are reasonable and applied consistently to all applicants. Thus, a competitive examination may cause you some uneasiness now, but it is your privilege and safeguard.

C. HOW ARE CIVIL SERVICE EXAMS DEVELOPED?

Examinations are carefully written by trained technicians who are specialists in the field known as "psychological measurement," in consultation with recognized authorities in the field of work that the test will cover. These experts recommend the subject matter areas or skills to be tested; only those knowledges or skills important to your success on the job are included. The most reliable books and source materials available are used as references. Together, the experts and technicians judge the difficulty level of the questions.

Test technicians know how to phrase questions so that the problem is clearly stated. Their ethics do not permit "trick" or "catch" questions. Questions may have been tried out on sample groups, or subjected to statistical analysis, to determine their usefulness.

Written tests are often used in combination with performance tests, ratings of training and experience, and oral interviews. All of these measures combine to form the best-known means of finding the right person for the right job.

II. HOW TO PASS THE WRITTEN TEST

A. NATURE OF THE EXAMINATION

To prepare intelligently for civil service examinations, you should know how they differ from school examinations you have taken. In school you were assigned certain definite pages to read or subjects to cover. The examination questions were quite detailed and usually emphasized memory. Civil service exams, on the other hand, try to discover your present ability to perform the duties of a position, plus your potentiality to learn these duties. In other words, a civil service exam attempts to predict how successful you will be. Questions cover such a broad area that they cannot be as minute and detailed as school exam questions.

In the public service similar kinds of work, or positions, are grouped together in one "class." This process is known as *position-classification*. All the positions in a class are paid according to the salary range for that class. One class title covers all of these positions, and they are all tested by the same examination.

B. FOUR BASIC STEPS

1) Study the announcement

How, then, can you know what subjects to study? Our best answer is: "Learn as much as possible about the class of positions for which you've applied." The exam will test the knowledge, skills and abilities needed to do the work.

Your most valuable source of information about the position you want is the official exam announcement. This announcement lists the training and experience qualifications. Check these standards and apply only if you come reasonably close to meeting them.

The brief description of the position in the examination announcement offers some clues to the subjects which will be tested. Think about the job itself. Review the duties in your mind. Can you perform them, or are there some in which you are rusty? Fill in the blank spots in your preparation.

Many jurisdictions preview the written test in the exam announcement by including a section called "Knowledge and Abilities Required," "Scope of the Examination," or some similar heading. Here you will find out specifically what fields will be tested.

2) Review your own background

Once you learn in general what the position is all about, and what you need to know to do the work, ask yourself which subjects you already know fairly well and which need improvement. You may wonder whether to concentrate on improving your strong areas or on building some background in your fields of weakness. When the announcement has specified "some knowledge" or "considerable knowledge," or has used adjectives like "beginning principles of..." or "advanced ... methods," you can get a clue as to the number and difficulty of questions to be asked in any given field. More questions, and hence broader coverage, would be included for those subjects which are more important in the work. Now weigh your strengths and weaknesses against the job requirements and prepare accordingly.

3) Determine the level of the position

Another way to tell how intensively you should prepare is to understand the level of the job for which you are applying. Is it the entering level? In other words, is this the position in which beginners in a field of work are hired? Or is it an intermediate or advanced level? Sometimes this is indicated by such words as "Junior" or "Senior" in the class title. Other jurisdictions use Roman numerals to designate the level – Clerk I, Clerk II, for example. The word "Supervisor" sometimes appears in the title. If the level is not indicated by the title, check the description of duties. Will you be working under very close supervision, or will you have responsibility for independent decisions in this work?

4) Choose appropriate study materials

Now that you know the subjects to be examined and the relative amount of each subject to be covered, you can choose suitable study materials. For beginning level jobs, or even advanced ones, if you have a pronounced weakness in some aspect of your training, read a modern, standard textbook in that field. Be sure it is up to date and has general coverage. Such books are normally available at your library, and the librarian will be glad to help you locate one. For entry-level positions, questions of appropriate difficulty are chosen – neither highly advanced questions, nor those too simple. Such questions require careful thought but not advanced training.

If the position for which you are applying is technical or advanced, you will read more advanced, specialized material. If you are already familiar with the basic principles of your field, elementary textbooks would waste your time. Concentrate on advanced textbooks and technical periodicals. Think through the concepts and review difficult problems in your field.

These are all general sources. You can get more ideas on your own initiative, following these leads. For example, training manuals and publications of the government agency which employs workers in your field can be useful, particularly for technical and professional positions. A letter or visit to the government department involved may result in more specific study suggestions, and certainly will provide you with a more definite idea of the exact nature of the position you are seeking.

III. KINDS OF TESTS

Tests are used for purposes other than measuring knowledge and ability to perform specified duties. For some positions, it is equally important to test ability to make adjustments to new situations or to profit from training. In others, basic mental abilities not dependent on information are essential. Questions which test these things may not appear as pertinent to the duties of the position as those which test for knowledge and information. Yet they are often highly important parts of a fair examination. For very general questions, it is almost impossible to help you direct your study efforts. What we can do is to point out some of the more common of these general abilities needed in public service positions and describe some typical questions.

1) General information

Broad, general information has been found useful for predicting job success in some kinds of work. This is tested in a variety of ways, from vocabulary lists to questions about current events. Basic background in some field of work, such as sociology or economics, may be sampled in a group of questions. Often these are principles which have become familiar to most persons through exposure rather than through formal training. It is difficult to advise you how to study for these questions; being alert to the world around you is our best suggestion.

2) Verbal ability

An example of an ability needed in many positions is verbal or language ability. Verbal ability is, in brief, the ability to use and understand words. Vocabulary and grammar tests are typical measures of this ability. Reading comprehension or paragraph interpretation questions are common in many kinds of civil service tests. You are given a paragraph of written material and asked to find its central meaning.

3) Numerical ability

Number skills can be tested by the familiar arithmetic problem, by checking paired lists of numbers to see which are alike and which are different, or by interpreting charts and graphs. In the latter test, a graph may be printed in the test booklet which you are asked to use as the basis for answering questions.

4) Observation

A popular test for law-enforcement positions is the observation test. A picture is shown to you for several minutes, then taken away. Questions about the picture test your ability to observe both details and larger elements.

5) Following directions

In many positions in the public service, the employee must be able to carry out written instructions dependably and accurately. You may be given a chart with several columns, each column listing a variety of information. The questions require you to carry out directions involving the information given in the chart.

6) Skills and aptitudes

Performance tests effectively measure some manual skills and aptitudes. When the skill is one in which you are trained, such as typing or shorthand, you can practice. These tests are often very much like those given in business school or high school courses. For many of the other skills and aptitudes, however, no short-time preparation can be made. Skills and abilities natural to you or that you have developed throughout your lifetime are being tested.

Many of the general questions just described provide all the data needed to answer the questions and ask you to use your reasoning ability to find the answers. Your best preparation for these tests, as well as for tests of facts and ideas, is to be at your physical and mental best. You, no doubt, have your own methods of getting into an exam-taking mood and keeping "in shape." The next section lists some ideas on this subject.

IV. KINDS OF QUESTIONS

Only rarely is the "essay" question, which you answer in narrative form, used in civil service tests. Civil service tests are usually of the short-answer type. Full instructions for answering these questions will be given to you at the examination. But in case this is your first experience with short-answer questions and separate answer sheets, here is what you need to know:

1) Multiple-choice Questions

Most popular of the short-answer questions is the "multiple choice" or "best answer" question. It can be used, for example, to test for factual knowledge, ability to solve problems or judgment in meeting situations found at work.

A multiple-choice question is normally one of three types—
- It can begin with an incomplete statement followed by several possible endings. You are to find the one ending which *best* completes the statement, although some of the others may not be entirely wrong.
- It can also be a complete statement in the form of a question which is answered by choosing one of the statements listed.

- It can be in the form of a problem – again you select the best answer.

Here is an example of a multiple-choice question with a discussion which should give you some clues as to the method for choosing the right answer:

When an employee has a complaint about his assignment, the action which will *best* help him overcome his difficulty is to
- A. discuss his difficulty with his coworkers
- B. take the problem to the head of the organization
- C. take the problem to the person who gave him the assignment
- D. say nothing to anyone about his complaint

In answering this question, you should study each of the choices to find which is best. Consider choice "A" – Certainly an employee may discuss his complaint with fellow employees, but no change or improvement can result, and the complaint remains unresolved. Choice "B" is a poor choice since the head of the organization probably does not know what assignment you have been given, and taking your problem to him is known as "going over the head" of the supervisor. The supervisor, or person who made the assignment, is the person who can clarify it or correct any injustice. Choice "C" is, therefore, correct. To say nothing, as in choice "D," is unwise. Supervisors have and interest in knowing the problems employees are facing, and the employee is seeking a solution to his problem.

2) True/False Questions

The "true/false" or "right/wrong" form of question is sometimes used. Here a complete statement is given. Your job is to decide whether the statement is right or wrong.

SAMPLE: A roaming cell-phone call to a nearby city costs less than a non-roaming call to a distant city.

This statement is wrong, or false, since roaming calls are more expensive.

This is not a complete list of all possible question forms, although most of the others are variations of these common types. You will always get complete directions for answering questions. Be sure you understand *how* to mark your answers – ask questions until you do.

V. RECORDING YOUR ANSWERS

Computer terminals are used more and more today for many different kinds of exams.

For an examination with very few applicants, you may be told to record your answers in the test booklet itself. Separate answer sheets are much more common. If this separate answer sheet is to be scored by machine – and this is often the case – it is highly important that you mark your answers correctly in order to get credit.

An electronic scoring machine is often used in civil service offices because of the speed with which papers can be scored. Machine-scored answer sheets must be marked with a pencil, which will be given to you. This pencil has a high graphite content which responds to the electronic scoring machine. As a matter of fact, stray dots may register as answers, so do not let your pencil rest on the answer sheet while you are pondering the correct answer. Also, if your pencil lead breaks or is otherwise defective, ask for another.

Since the answer sheet will be dropped in a slot in the scoring machine, be careful not to bend the corners or get the paper crumpled.

The answer sheet normally has five vertical columns of numbers, with 30 numbers to a column. These numbers correspond to the question numbers in your test booklet. After each number, going across the page are four or five pairs of dotted lines. These short dotted lines have small letters or numbers above them. The first two pairs may also have a "T" or "F" above the letters. This indicates that the first two pairs only are to be used if the questions are of the true-false type. If the questions are multiple choice, disregard the "T" and "F" and pay attention only to the small letters or numbers.

Answer your questions in the manner of the sample that follows:

32. The largest city in the United States is
    A. Washington, D.C.
    B. New York City
    C. Chicago
    D. Detroit
    E. San Francisco

1) Choose the answer you think is best. (New York City is the largest, so "B" is correct.)
2) Find the row of dotted lines numbered the same as the question you are answering. (Find row number 32)
3) Find the pair of dotted lines corresponding to the answer. (Find the pair of lines under the mark "B.")
4) Make a solid black mark between the dotted lines.

VI. BEFORE THE TEST

Common sense will help you find procedures to follow to get ready for an examination. Too many of us, however, overlook these sensible measures. Indeed, nervousness and fatigue have been found to be the most serious reasons why applicants fail to do their best on civil service tests. Here is a list of reminders:

- Begin your preparation early – Don't wait until the last minute to go scurrying around for books and materials or to find out what the position is all about.
- Prepare continuously – An hour a night for a week is better than an all-night cram session. This has been definitely established. What is more, a night a week for a month will return better dividends than crowding your study into a shorter period of time.
- Locate the place of the exam – You have been sent a notice telling you when and where to report for the examination. If the location is in a different town or otherwise unfamiliar to you, it would be well to inquire the best route and learn something about the building.
- Relax the night before the test – Allow your mind to rest. Do not study at all that night. Plan some mild recreation or diversion; then go to bed early and get a good night's sleep.
- Get up early enough to make a leisurely trip to the place for the test – This way unforeseen events, traffic snarls, unfamiliar buildings, etc. will not upset you.
- Dress comfortably – A written test is not a fashion show. You will be known by number and not by name, so wear something comfortable.

- Leave excess paraphernalia at home – Shopping bags and odd bundles will get in your way. You need bring only the items mentioned in the official notice you received; usually everything you need is provided. Do not bring reference books to the exam. They will only confuse those last minutes and be taken away from you when in the test room.
- Arrive somewhat ahead of time – If because of transportation schedules you must get there very early, bring a newspaper or magazine to take your mind off yourself while waiting.
- Locate the examination room – When you have found the proper room, you will be directed to the seat or part of the room where you will sit. Sometimes you are given a sheet of instructions to read while you are waiting. Do not fill out any forms until you are told to do so; just read them and be prepared.
- Relax and prepare to listen to the instructions
- If you have any physical problem that may keep you from doing your best, be sure to tell the test administrator. If you are sick or in poor health, you really cannot do your best on the exam. You can come back and take the test some other time.

VII. AT THE TEST

The day of the test is here and you have the test booklet in your hand. The temptation to get going is very strong. Caution! There is more to success than knowing the right answers. You must know how to identify your papers and understand variations in the type of short-answer question used in this particular examination. Follow these suggestions for maximum results from your efforts:

1) Cooperate with the monitor

The test administrator has a duty to create a situation in which you can be as much at ease as possible. He will give instructions, tell you when to begin, check to see that you are marking your answer sheet correctly, and so on. He is not there to guard you, although he will see that your competitors do not take unfair advantage. He wants to help you do your best.

2) Listen to all instructions

Don't jump the gun! Wait until you understand all directions. In most civil service tests you get more time than you need to answer the questions. So don't be in a hurry. Read each word of instructions until you clearly understand the meaning. Study the examples, listen to all announcements and follow directions. Ask questions if you do not understand what to do.

3) Identify your papers

Civil service exams are usually identified by number only. You will be assigned a number; you must not put your name on your test papers. Be sure to copy your number correctly. Since more than one exam may be given, copy your exact examination title.

4) Plan your time

Unless you are told that a test is a "speed" or "rate of work" test, speed itself is usually not important. Time enough to answer all the questions will be provided, but this does not mean that you have all day. An overall time limit has been set. Divide the total time (in minutes) by the number of questions to determine the approximate time you have for each question.

5) Do not linger over difficult questions

If you come across a difficult question, mark it with a paper clip (useful to have along) and come back to it when you have been through the booklet. One caution if you do this – be sure to skip a number on your answer sheet as well. Check often to be sure that you have not lost your place and that you are marking in the row numbered the same as the question you are answering.

6) Read the questions

Be sure you know what the question asks! Many capable people are unsuccessful because they failed to *read* the questions correctly.

7) Answer all questions

Unless you have been instructed that a penalty will be deducted for incorrect answers, it is better to guess than to omit a question.

8) Speed tests

It is often better NOT to guess on speed tests. It has been found that on timed tests people are tempted to spend the last few seconds before time is called in marking answers at random – without even reading them – in the hope of picking up a few extra points. To discourage this practice, the instructions may warn you that your score will be "corrected" for guessing. That is, a penalty will be applied. The incorrect answers will be deducted from the correct ones, or some other penalty formula will be used.

9) Review your answers

If you finish before time is called, go back to the questions you guessed or omitted to give them further thought. Review other answers if you have time.

10) Return your test materials

If you are ready to leave before others have finished or time is called, take ALL your materials to the monitor and leave quietly. Never take any test material with you. The monitor can discover whose papers are not complete, and taking a test booklet may be grounds for disqualification.

VIII. EXAMINATION TECHNIQUES

1) Read the general instructions carefully. These are usually printed on the first page of the exam booklet. As a rule, these instructions refer to the timing of the examination; the fact that you should not start work until the signal and must stop work at a signal, etc. If there are any *special* instructions, such as a choice of questions to be answered, make sure that you note this instruction carefully.

2) When you are ready to start work on the examination, that is as soon as the signal has been given, read the instructions to each question booklet, underline any key words or phrases, such as *least, best, outline, describe* and the like. In this way you will tend to answer as requested rather than discover on reviewing your paper that you *listed without describing*, that you selected the *worst* choice rather than the *best* choice, etc.

3) If the examination is of the objective or multiple-choice type – that is, each question will also give a series of possible answers: A, B, C or D, and you are called upon to select the best answer and write the letter next to that answer on your answer paper – it is advisable to start answering each question in turn. There may be anywhere from 50 to 100 such questions in the three or four hours allotted and you can see how much time would be taken if you read through all the questions before beginning to answer any. Furthermore, if you come across a question or group of questions which you know would be difficult to answer, it would undoubtedly affect your handling of all the other questions.

4) If the examination is of the essay type and contains but a few questions, it is a moot point as to whether you should read all the questions before starting to answer any one. Of course, if you are given a choice – say five out of seven and the like – then it is essential to read all the questions so you can eliminate the two that are most difficult. If, however, you are asked to answer all the questions, there may be danger in trying to answer the easiest one first because you may find that you will spend too much time on it. The best technique is to answer the first question, then proceed to the second, etc.

5) Time your answers. Before the exam begins, write down the time it started, then add the time allowed for the examination and write down the time it must be completed, then divide the time available somewhat as follows:
    - If 3-1/2 hours are allowed, that would be 210 minutes. If you have 80 objective-type questions, that would be an average of 2-1/2 minutes per question. Allow yourself no more than 2 minutes per question, or a total of 160 minutes, which will permit about 50 minutes to review.
    - If for the time allotment of 210 minutes there are 7 essay questions to answer, that would average about 30 minutes a question. Give yourself only 25 minutes per question so that you have about 35 minutes to review.

6) The most important instruction is to *read each question* and make sure you know what is wanted. The second most important instruction is to *time yourself properly* so that you answer every question. The third most important instruction is to *answer every question*. Guess if you have to but include something for each question. Remember that you will receive no credit for a blank and will probably receive some credit if you write something in answer to an essay question. If you guess a letter – say "B" for a multiple-choice question – you may have guessed right. If you leave a blank as an answer to a multiple-choice question, the examiners may respect your feelings but it will not add a point to your score. Some exams may penalize you for wrong answers, so in such cases *only*, you may not want to guess unless you have some basis for your answer.

7) Suggestions
   a. Objective-type questions
      1. Examine the question booklet for proper sequence of pages and questions
      2. Read all instructions carefully
      3. Skip any question which seems too difficult; return to it after all other questions have been answered
      4. Apportion your time properly; do not spend too much time on any single question or group of questions

5. Note and underline key words – *all, most, fewest, least, best, worst, same, opposite,* etc.
6. Pay particular attention to negatives
7. Note unusual option, e.g., unduly long, short, complex, different or similar in content to the body of the question
8. Observe the use of "hedging" words – *probably, may, most likely,* etc.
9. Make sure that your answer is put next to the same number as the question
10. Do not second-guess unless you have good reason to believe the second answer is definitely more correct
11. Cross out original answer if you decide another answer is more accurate; do not erase until you are ready to hand your paper in
12. Answer all questions; guess unless instructed otherwise
13. Leave time for review

b. Essay questions
1. Read each question carefully
2. Determine exactly what is wanted. Underline key words or phrases.
3. Decide on outline or paragraph answer
4. Include many different points and elements unless asked to develop any one or two points or elements
5. Show impartiality by giving pros and cons unless directed to select one side only
6. Make and write down any assumptions you find necessary to answer the questions
7. Watch your English, grammar, punctuation and choice of words
8. Time your answers; don't crowd material

8) Answering the essay question

Most essay questions can be answered by framing the specific response around several key words or ideas. Here are a few such key words or ideas:

M's: manpower, materials, methods, money, management
P's: purpose, program, policy, plan, procedure, practice, problems, pitfalls, personnel, public relations

a. Six basic steps in handling problems:
1. Preliminary plan and background development
2. Collect information, data and facts
3. Analyze and interpret information, data and facts
4. Analyze and develop solutions as well as make recommendations
5. Prepare report and sell recommendations
6. Install recommendations and follow up effectiveness

b. Pitfalls to avoid
1. *Taking things for granted* – A statement of the situation does not necessarily imply that each of the elements is necessarily true; for example, a complaint may be invalid and biased so that all that can be taken for granted is that a complaint has been registered

2. *Considering only one side of a situation* – Wherever possible, indicate several alternatives and then point out the reasons you selected the best one
3. *Failing to indicate follow up* – Whenever your answer indicates action on your part, make certain that you will take proper follow-up action to see how successful your recommendations, procedures or actions turn out to be
4. *Taking too long in answering any single question* – Remember to time your answers properly

IX. AFTER THE TEST

Scoring procedures differ in detail among civil service jurisdictions although the general principles are the same. Whether the papers are hand-scored or graded by machine we have described, they are nearly always graded by number. That is, the person who marks the paper knows only the number – never the name – of the applicant. Not until all the papers have been graded will they be matched with names. If other tests, such as training and experience or oral interview ratings have been given, scores will be combined. Different parts of the examination usually have different weights. For example, the written test might count 60 percent of the final grade, and a rating of training and experience 40 percent. In many jurisdictions, veterans will have a certain number of points added to their grades.

After the final grade has been determined, the names are placed in grade order and an eligible list is established. There are various methods for resolving ties between those who get the same final grade – probably the most common is to place first the name of the person whose application was received first. Job offers are made from the eligible list in the order the names appear on it. You will be notified of your grade and your rank as soon as all these computations have been made. This will be done as rapidly as possible.

People who are found to meet the requirements in the announcement are called "eligibles." Their names are put on a list of eligible candidates. An eligible's chances of getting a job depend on how high he stands on this list and how fast agencies are filling jobs from the list.

When a job is to be filled from a list of eligibles, the agency asks for the names of people on the list of eligibles for that job. When the civil service commission receives this request, it sends to the agency the names of the three people highest on this list. Or, if the job to be filled has specialized requirements, the office sends the agency the names of the top three persons who meet these requirements from the general list.

The appointing officer makes a choice from among the three people whose names were sent to him. If the selected person accepts the appointment, the names of the others are put back on the list to be considered for future openings.

That is the rule in hiring from all kinds of eligible lists, whether they are for typist, carpenter, chemist, or something else. For every vacancy, the appointing officer has his choice of any one of the top three eligibles on the list. This explains why the person whose name is on top of the list sometimes does not get an appointment when some of the persons lower on the list do. If the appointing officer chooses the second or third eligible, the No. 1 eligible does not get a job at once, but stays on the list until he is appointed or the list is terminated.

X. HOW TO PASS THE INTERVIEW TEST

The examination for which you applied requires an oral interview test. You have already taken the written test and you are now being called for the interview test – the final part of the formal examination.

You may think that it is not possible to prepare for an interview test and that there are no procedures to follow during an interview. Our purpose is to point out some things you can do in advance that will help you and some good rules to follow and pitfalls to avoid while you are being interviewed.

What is an interview supposed to test?

The written examination is designed to test the technical knowledge and competence of the candidate; the oral is designed to evaluate intangible qualities, not readily measured otherwise, and to establish a list showing the relative fitness of each candidate – as measured against his competitors – for the position sought. Scoring is not on the basis of "right" and "wrong," but on a sliding scale of values ranging from "not passable" to "outstanding." As a matter of fact, it is possible to achieve a relatively low score without a single "incorrect" answer because of evident weakness in the qualities being measured.

Occasionally, an examination may consist entirely of an oral test – either an individual or a group oral. In such cases, information is sought concerning the technical knowledges and abilities of the candidate, since there has been no written examination for this purpose. More commonly, however, an oral test is used to supplement a written examination.

Who conducts interviews?

The composition of oral boards varies among different jurisdictions. In nearly all, a representative of the personnel department serves as chairman. One of the members of the board may be a representative of the department in which the candidate would work. In some cases, "outside experts" are used, and, frequently, a businessman or some other representative of the general public is asked to serve. Labor and management or other special groups may be represented. The aim is to secure the services of experts in the appropriate field.

However the board is composed, it is a good idea (and not at all improper or unethical) to ascertain in advance of the interview who the members are and what groups they represent. When you are introduced to them, you will have some idea of their backgrounds and interests, and at least you will not stutter and stammer over their names.

What should be done before the interview?

While knowledge about the board members is useful and takes some of the surprise element out of the interview, there is other preparation which is more substantive. It *is* possible to prepare for an oral interview – in several ways:

1) Keep a copy of your application and review it carefully before the interview

This may be the only document before the oral board, and the starting point of the interview. Know what education and experience you have listed there, and the sequence and dates of all of it. Sometimes the board will ask you to review the highlights of your experience for them; you should not have to hem and haw doing it.

2) Study the class specification and the examination announcement

Usually, the oral board has one or both of these to guide them. The qualities, characteristics or knowledges required by the position sought are stated in these documents. They offer valuable clues as to the nature of the oral interview. For example, if the job involves supervisory responsibilities, the announcement will usually indicate that knowledge of modern supervisory methods and the qualifications of the candidate as a supervisor will be tested. If so, you can expect such questions, frequently in the form of a hypothetical situation which you are expected to solve. NEVER go into an oral without knowledge of the duties and responsibilities of the job you seek.

3) Think through each qualification required

Try to visualize the kind of questions you would ask if you were a board member. How well could you answer them? Try especially to appraise your own knowledge and background in each area, *measured against the job sought*, and identify any areas in which you are weak. Be critical and realistic – do not flatter yourself.

4) Do some general reading in areas in which you feel you may be weak

For example, if the job involves supervision and your past experience has NOT, some general reading in supervisory methods and practices, particularly in the field of human relations, might be useful. Do NOT study agency procedures or detailed manuals. The oral board will be testing your understanding and capacity, not your memory.

5) Get a good night's sleep and watch your general health and mental attitude

You will want a clear head at the interview. Take care of a cold or any other minor ailment, and of course, no hangovers.

What should be done on the day of the interview?

Now comes the day of the interview itself. Give yourself plenty of time to get there. Plan to arrive somewhat ahead of the scheduled time, particularly if your appointment is in the fore part of the day. If a previous candidate fails to appear, the board might be ready for you a bit early. By early afternoon an oral board is almost invariably behind schedule if there are many candidates, and you may have to wait. Take along a book or magazine to read, or your application to review, but leave any extraneous material in the waiting room when you go in for your interview. In any event, relax and compose yourself.

The matter of dress is important. The board is forming impressions about you – from your experience, your manners, your attitude, and your appearance. Give your personal appearance careful attention. Dress your best, but not your flashiest. Choose conservative, appropriate clothing, and be sure it is immaculate. This is a business interview, and your appearance should indicate that you regard it as such. Besides, being well groomed and properly dressed will help boost your confidence.

Sooner or later, someone will call your name and escort you into the interview room. *This is it*. From here on you are on your own. It is too late for any more preparation. But remember, you asked for this opportunity to prove your fitness, and you are here because your request was granted.

What happens when you go in?

The usual sequence of events will be as follows: The clerk (who is often the board stenographer) will introduce you to the chairman of the oral board, who will introduce you to the other members of the board. Acknowledge the introductions before you sit down. Do not be surprised if you find a microphone facing you or a stenotypist sitting by. Oral interviews are usually recorded in the event of an appeal or other review.

Usually the chairman of the board will open the interview by reviewing the highlights of your education and work experience from your application – primarily for the benefit of the other members of the board, as well as to get the material into the record. Do not interrupt or comment unless there is an error or significant misinterpretation; if that is the case, do not hesitate. But do not quibble about insignificant matters. Also, he will usually ask you some question about your education, experience or your present job – partly to get you to start talking and to establish the interviewing "rapport." He may start the actual questioning, or turn it over to one of the other members. Frequently, each member undertakes the questioning on a particular area, one in which he is perhaps most competent, so you can expect each member to participate in the examination. Because time is limited, you may also expect some rather abrupt switches in the direction the questioning takes, so do not be upset by it. Normally, a board member will not pursue a single line of questioning unless he discovers a particular strength or weakness.

After each member has participated, the chairman will usually ask whether any member has any further questions, then will ask you if you have anything you wish to add. Unless you are expecting this question, it may floor you. Worse, it may start you off on an extended, extemporaneous speech. The board is not usually seeking more information. The question is principally to offer you a last opportunity to present further qualifications or to indicate that you have nothing to add. So, if you feel that a significant qualification or characteristic has been overlooked, it is proper to point it out in a sentence or so. Do not compliment the board on the thoroughness of their examination – they have been sketchy, and you know it. If you wish, merely say, "No thank you, I have nothing further to add." This is a point where you can "talk yourself out" of a good impression or fail to present an important bit of information. Remember, *you close the interview yourself.*

The chairman will then say, "That is all, Mr. _____, thank you." Do not be startled; the interview is over, and quicker than you think. Thank him, gather your belongings and take your leave. Save your sigh of relief for the other side of the door.

How to put your best foot forward

Throughout this entire process, you may feel that the board individually and collectively is trying to pierce your defenses, seek out your hidden weaknesses and embarrass and confuse you. Actually, this is not true. They are obliged to make an appraisal of your qualifications for the job you are seeking, and they want to see you in your best light. Remember, they must interview all candidates and a non-cooperative candidate may become a failure in spite of their best efforts to bring out his qualifications. Here are 15 suggestions that will help you:

1) Be natural – Keep your attitude confident, not cocky

If you are not confident that you can do the job, do not expect the board to be. Do not apologize for your weaknesses, try to bring out your strong points. The board is interested in a positive, not negative, presentation. Cockiness will antagonize any board member and make him wonder if you are covering up a weakness by a false show of strength.

2) Get comfortable, but don't lounge or sprawl

Sit erectly but not stiffly. A careless posture may lead the board to conclude that you are careless in other things, or at least that you are not impressed by the importance of the occasion. Either conclusion is natural, even if incorrect. Do not fuss with your clothing, a pencil or an ashtray. Your hands may occasionally be useful to emphasize a point; do not let them become a point of distraction.

3) Do not wisecrack or make small talk

This is a serious situation, and your attitude should show that you consider it as such. Further, the time of the board is limited – they do not want to waste it, and neither should you.

4) Do not exaggerate your experience or abilities

In the first place, from information in the application or other interviews and sources, the board may know more about you than you think. Secondly, you probably will not get away with it. An experienced board is rather adept at spotting such a situation, so do not take the chance.

5) If you know a board member, do not make a point of it, yet do not hide it

Certainly you are not fooling him, and probably not the other members of the board. Do not try to take advantage of your acquaintanceship – it will probably do you little good.

6) Do not dominate the interview

Let the board do that. They will give you the clues – do not assume that you have to do all the talking. Realize that the board has a number of questions to ask you, and do not try to take up all the interview time by showing off your extensive knowledge of the answer to the first one.

7) Be attentive

You only have 20 minutes or so, and you should keep your attention at its sharpest throughout. When a member is addressing a problem or question to you, give him your undivided attention. Address your reply principally to him, but do not exclude the other board members.

8) Do not interrupt

A board member may be stating a problem for you to analyze. He will ask you a question when the time comes. Let him state the problem, and wait for the question.

9) Make sure you understand the question

Do not try to answer until you are sure what the question is. If it is not clear, restate it in your own words or ask the board member to clarify it for you. However, do not haggle about minor elements.

10) Reply promptly but not hastily

A common entry on oral board rating sheets is "candidate responded readily," or "candidate hesitated in replies." Respond as promptly and quickly as you can, but do not jump to a hasty, ill-considered answer.

11) Do not be peremptory in your answers

A brief answer is proper – but do not fire your answer back. That is a losing game from your point of view. The board member can probably ask questions much faster than you can answer them.

12) Do not try to create the answer you think the board member wants

He is interested in what kind of mind you have and how it works – not in playing games. Furthermore, he can usually spot this practice and will actually grade you down on it.

13) Do not switch sides in your reply merely to agree with a board member

Frequently, a member will take a contrary position merely to draw you out and to see if you are willing and able to defend your point of view. Do not start a debate, yet do not surrender a good position. If a position is worth taking, it is worth defending.

14) Do not be afraid to admit an error in judgment if you are shown to be wrong
The board knows that you are forced to reply without any opportunity for careful consideration. Your answer may be demonstrably wrong. If so, admit it and get on with the interview.

15) Do not dwell at length on your present job
The opening question may relate to your present assignment. Answer the question but do not go into an extended discussion. You are being examined for a *new* job, not your present one. As a matter of fact, try to phrase ALL your answers in terms of the job for which you are being examined.

Basis of Rating
Probably you will forget most of these "do's" and "don'ts" when you walk into the oral interview room. Even remembering them all will not ensure you a passing grade. Perhaps you did not have the qualifications in the first place. But remembering them will help you to put your best foot forward, without treading on the toes of the board members.

Rumor and popular opinion to the contrary notwithstanding, an oral board wants you to make the best appearance possible. They know you are under pressure – but they also want to see how you respond to it as a guide to what your reaction would be under the pressures of the job you seek. They will be influenced by the degree of poise you display, the personal traits you show and the manner in which you respond.

ABOUT THIS BOOK

This book contains tests divided into Examination Sections. Go through each test, answering every question in the margin. We have also attached a sample answer sheet at the back of the book that can be removed and used. At the end of each test look at the answer key and check your answers. On the ones you got wrong, look at the right answer choice and learn. Do not fill in the answers first. Do not memorize the questions and answers, but understand the answer and principles involved. On your test, the questions will likely be different from the samples. Questions are changed and new ones added. If you understand these past questions you should have success with any changes that arise. Tests may consist of several types of questions. We have additional books on each subject should more study be advisable or necessary for you. Finally, the more you study, the better prepared you will be. This book is intended to be the last thing you study before you walk into the examination room. Prior study of relevant texts is also recommended. NLC publishes some of these in our Fundamental Series. Knowledge and good sense are important factors in passing your exam. Good luck also helps. So now study this Passbook, absorb the material contained within and take that knowledge into the examination. Then do your best to pass that exam.

EXAMINATION SECTION

EXAMINATION SECTION
TEST 1

DIRECTIONS: Each question or incomplete statement is followed by several suggested answers or completions. Select the one that BEST answers the question or completes the statement. *PRINT THE LETTER OF THE CORRECT ANSWER IN THE SPACE AT THE RIGHT.*

1. The combustion efficiency of a boiler can be determined with a CO_2 indicator and the   1.____

   A. under fire draft
   B. boiler room humidity
   C. flue gas temperature
   D. outside air temperature

2. A quick, practical method of determining if the cast-iron waste pipe delivered to a job has been damaged in transit is to   2.____

   A. hydraulically test it
   B. "ring" each length with a hammer
   C. drop each length to see whether it breaks
   D. visually examine the pipe for cracks

3. An electrostatic precipitator is used to   3.____

   A. filter the air supply
   B. remove sludge from the fuel oil
   C. remove particles from the fuel gas
   D. supply samples for an Orsat analysis

4. The PRIMARY cause of cracking and spalling of refractory lining in the furnace of a steam generator is *most likely* due to   4.____

   A. continuous over-firing of boiler
   B. slag accumulation on furnace walls
   C. change in fuel from solid to liquid
   D. uneven heating and cooling within the refractory brick

5. The term "effective temperature" in air conditioning means   5.____

   A. the dry bulb temperature
   B. the average of the wet and dry bulb temperatures
   C. the square root of the product of wet and dry bulb temperatures
   D. an arbitrary index combining the effects of temperature, humidity, and movement

6. The piping in all buildings having dual water distribution systems should be identified by a color coding of _____ for potable water lines and _____ for non-potable water lines.   6.____

   A. green; red
   B. green; yellow
   C. yellow; green
   D. yellow; red

7. The breaking of a component of a machine subjected to excessive vibration is called   7.____

   A. tensile failure
   B. fatigue failure
   C. caustic embrittlement
   D. amplitude failure

8. The TWO MOST important factors to be considered in selecting fans for ventilating systems are 8._____

    A. noise and efficiency
    B. space available and weight
    C. first cost and dimensional bulk
    D. construction and arrangement of drive

9. In the modern power plant deaerator, air is removed from water to 9._____

    A. reduce heat losses in the heaters
    B. reduce corrosion of boiler steel due to the air
    C. reduce the load of the main condenser air pumps
    D. prevent pumps from becoming vapor bound

10. The abbreviations BOD, COD, and DO are associated with 10._____

    A. flue gas analysis   B. air pollution control
    C. boiler water treatment   D. water pollution control

11. The piping of a newly installed drainage system should be tested upon completion of the rough plumbing with a head of water of NOT LESS THAN _____ feet. 11._____

    A. 10   B. 15   C. 20   D. 25

12. Of the following statements concerning aquastats, the one which is CORRECT is: 12._____

    A. Aquastats may be obtained with either a narrow or wide range of settings
    B. Aquastats have a mercury tube switch which is controlled by the stack switch
    C. An aquastat is a device used to shut down the burner in the event of low water in the boiler
    D. An aquastat should be located about 4 inches above the normal water line of the boiler

13. The SAFEST way to protect the domestic water supply from contamination by sewage or non-potable water is to insert 13._____

    A. air gaps
    B. swing connections
    C. double check valves
    D. tanks with overhead discharge

14. The MAIN function of a back-pressure valve which is sometimes found in the connection between a water drain pipe and the sewer system is to 14._____

    A. equalize the pressure between the drain pipe and the sewer
    B. prevent sewer water from flowing into the drain pipe
    C. provide pressure to enable waste to reach the sewer
    D. make sure that there is not too much water pressure in the sewer line

15. Boiler water is neutral if its pH value is 15._____

    A. 0   B. 1   C. 7   D. 14

16. A domestic hot water mixing or tempering valve should be preceded in the hot water line by a

    A. strainer   B. foot valve
    C. check valve   D. steam trap

16.____

17. Between a steam boiler and its safety valve there should be

    A. no valve of any type
    B. a gate valve of the same size as the safety valve
    C. a swing check valve of at least the same size as the safety valve
    D. a cock having a clear opening equal in area to the pipe connecting the boiler and safety valve

17.____

18. A diagram of horizontal plumbing drainage lines should have cleanouts shown

    A. at least every 25 feet
    B. at least every 100 feet
    C. wherever a basin is located
    D. wherever a change in direction occurs

18.____

19. When a Bourdon gauge is used to measure steam pressures, some form of siphon or water seal must be maintained.
The reason for this is to

    A. obtain "absolute" pressure readings
    B. prevent steam from entering the gage
    C. prevent condensate from entering the gage
    D. obtain readings below atmospheric pressure

19.____

20. In a closed heat exchanger, oil is cooled by condensate which is to be returned to a boiler. In order to avoid the possibility of contaminating the condensate with oil should a tube fail in the oil cooler, it would be good practice to

    A. cool the oil by air instead of water
    B. treat the condensate with an oil solvent
    C. keep the oil pressure in the exchanger higher than the water pressure
    D. keep the water pressure in the exchanger higher than the oil pressure

20.____

21. A radiator thermostatic trap is used on a vacuum return type of heating system to

    A. release the pocketed air only
    B. reduce the amount of condensate
    C. maintain a predetermined radiator water level
    D. prevent the return of live steam to the return line

21.____

22. According to the color coding of piping, fire protection piping should be painted

    A. green   B. yellow   C. purple   D. red

22.____

23. The MAIN purpose of a standpipe system is to

    A. supply the roof water tank
    B. provide water for firefighting

23.____

C. circulate water for the heating system
D. provide adequate pressure for the water supply

24. The name "Saybolt" is associated with the measurement of

    A. viscosity
    B. Btu content
    C. octane rating
    D. temperature

25. Recirculation of conditioned air in an air-conditioned building is done MAINLY to

    A. reduce refrigeration tonnage required
    B. increase room entrophy
    C. increase air specific humidity
    D. reduce room temperature below the dewpoint

26. In a plumbing installation, vent pipes are GENERALLY used to

    A. prevent the loss of water seal from traps by evaporation
    B. prevent the loss of water seal due to several causes other than evaporation
    C. act as an additional path for liquids to flow through during normal use of a plumbing fixture
    D. prevent the backflow of water in a cross-connection between a drinking water line and a sewage line

27. The designation "150 W" cast on the bonnet of a gate valve is an indication of the

    A. water working temperature
    B. water working pressure
    C. area of the opening in square inches
    D. weight of the valve in pounds

28. In the city, the size soil pipe necessary in a sewage drainage system is determined by the

    A. legal occupancy of the building
    B. vertical height of the soil line
    C. number of restrooms connected to the soil line
    D. number of "fixture units" connected to the soil line

29. Fins or other extended surfaces are used on heat exchanger tubes when

    A. the exchanger is a water-to-water exchanger
    B. water is on one side of the tube and condensing steam on the other side
    C. the surface coefficient of heat transfer on both sides of the tube is high
    D. the surface coefficient of heat transfer on one side of the tube is low compared to the coefficient on the other side of the tube

30. A fusible plug may be put in a fire tube boiler as an emergency device to indicate low water level. The fusible plug is installed so that under normal operating conditions,

    A. both sides are exposed to steam
    B. one side is exposed to water and the other side to steam
    C. one side is exposed to steam and the other side to hot gases
    D. one side is exposed to the water and the other side to hot gases

31. Extra strong wrought-iron pipe, as compared to standard wrought-iron pipe of the same nominal size, has

    A. the same outside diameter but a smaller inside diameter
    B. the same inside diameter but a larger outside diameter
    C. a larger outside diameter and a smaller inside diameter
    D. larger inside and outside diameters

31._____

32. Fans may be rated on a dynamic or a static efficiency basis. The dynamic efficiency would *probably* be

    A. lower in value because of the energy absorbed by the air velocity
    B. the same as the static in the case of centrifugal blowers running at various speeds
    C. the same as the static in the case of axial flow blowers running at various speeds
    D. higher in value than the static

32._____

33. The function of the stack relay in an oil burner installation is to

    A. regulate the draft over the fire
    B. regulate the flow of fuel oil to the burner
    C. stop the motor if the oil has not ignited
    D. stop the motor if the water or steam pressure is too high

33._____

34. The type of centrifugal pump which is inherently balanced for hydraulic thrust is the

    A. double suction impeller type
    B. single suction impeller type
    C. single stage type
    D. multistage type

34._____

35. The specifications for a job using sheet lead calls for "4-lb. sheet lead."
    This means that each sheet should weigh

    A. 4 lbs.   B. 4 lbs. per square
    C. 4 lbs. per square foot   D. 4 lbs. per cubic inch

35._____

36. The total cooling load design conditions for a building are divided for convenience into two components.
    These are:

    A. infiltration and radiation
    B. sensible heat and latent heat
    C. wet and dry bulb temperatures
    D. solar heat gain and moisture transfer

36._____

37. The function of a Hartford loop used on some steam boilers is to

    A. limit boiler steam pressure
    B. limit temperature of the steam
    C. prevent high water levels in the boiler
    D. prevent back flow of water from the boiler into the return main

37._____

38. Vibration from a ventilating blower can be prevented from being transmitted to the duct work by

   A. installing straighteners in the duct
   B. throttling the air supply to the blower
   C. bolting the blower tightly to the duct
   D. installing a canvas sleeve at the blower outlet

38.____

39. A specification states that access panels to suspended ceiling will be of metal. The MAIN reason for providing access panels is to

   A. improve the insulation of the ceiling
   B. improve the appearance of the ceiling
   C. make it easier to construct the building
   D. make it easier to maintain the building

39.____

40. A plumber on a job reports that the steamfitter has installed a 3" steam line in a location at which the plans show the house trap. On inspecting the job, you should

   A. tell the steamfitter to remove the steam line
   B. study the condition to see if the house trap can be relocated
   C. tell the plumber and steamfitter to work it out between themselves and then report to you
   D. tell the plumber to find another location for the trap because the steamfitter has already completed his work

40.____

41. In the installation of any heating system, the MOST important consideration is that

   A. all elements be made of a good grade of cast iron
   B. all radiators and connectors be mounted horizontally
   C. the smallest velocity of flow of heating medium be used
   D. there be proper clearance between hot surfaces and surrounding combustible material

41.____

42. Which one of the following is the PRIMARY object in drawing up a set of specifications for materials to be purchased?

   A. Control of quality
   B. Outline of intended use
   C. Establishment of standard sizes
   D. Location and method of inspection.

42.____

43. The drawing which should be used as a LEGAL reference when checking completed construction work is the _____ drawing.

   A. contract   B. assembly
   C. working or shop   D. preliminary

43.____

Questions 44-50.

DIRECTIONS: Questions 44 through 50 refer to the plumbing drawing shown below.

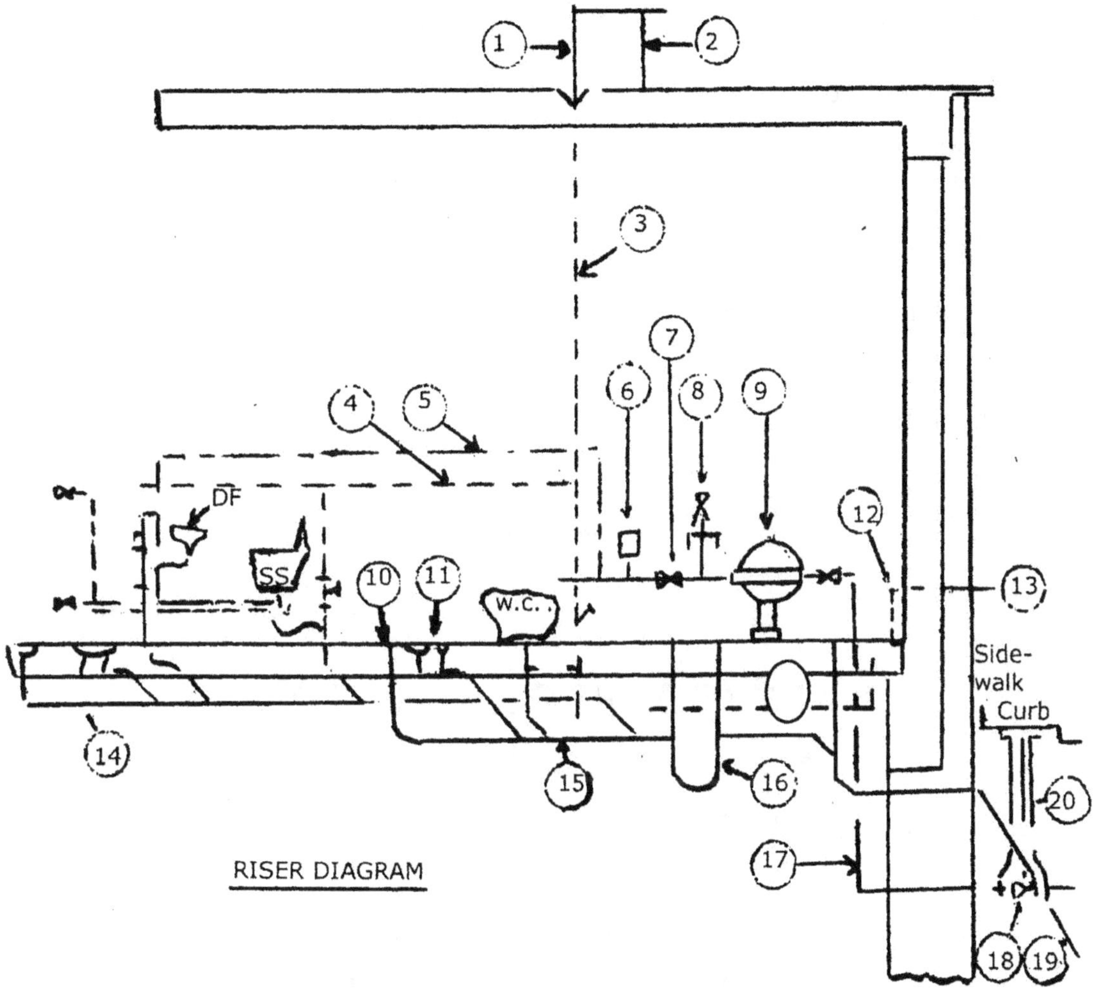

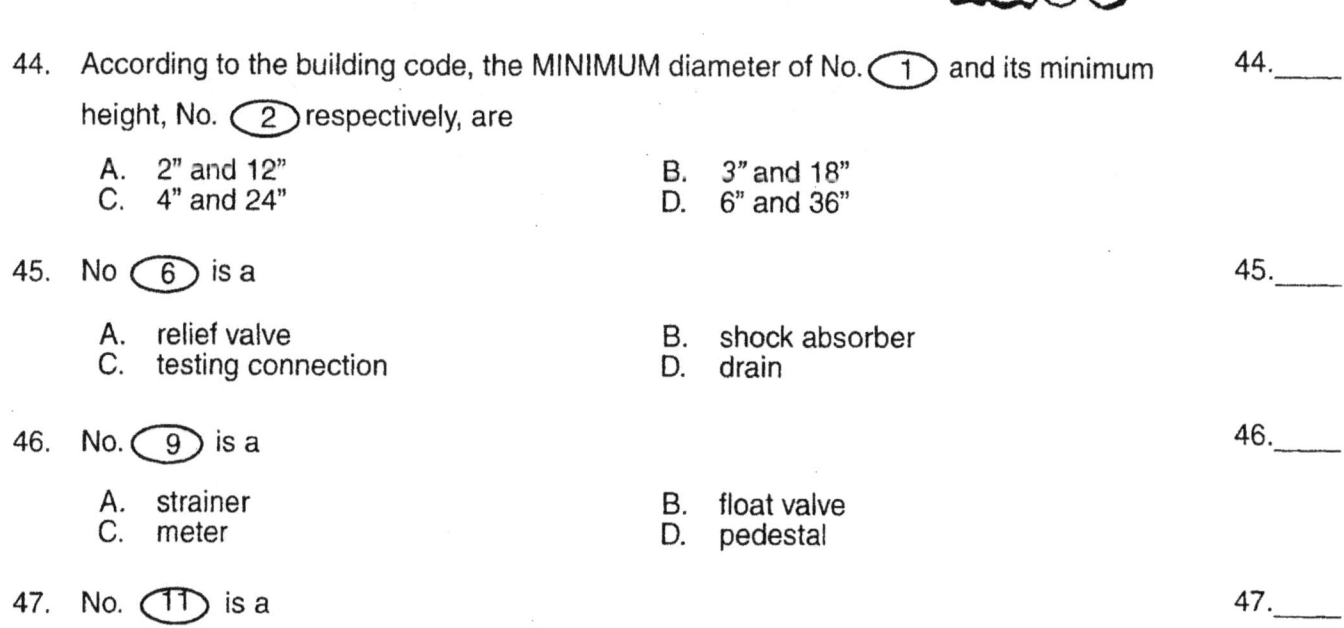

RISER DIAGRAM

44. According to the building code, the MINIMUM diameter of No. ① and its minimum height, No. ② respectively, are

    A. 2" and 12"
    B. 3" and 18"
    C. 4" and 24"
    D. 6" and 36"

44.____

45. No. ⑥ is a

    A. relief valve
    B. shock absorber
    C. testing connection
    D. drain

45.____

46. No. ⑨ is a

    A. strainer
    B. float valve
    C. meter
    D. pedestal

46.____

47. No. ⑪ is a

    A. floor drain
    B. cleanout
    C. trap
    D. vent connection

47.____

48. No. ⑬ is a

   A. standpipe
   C. sprinkler head
   B. air inlet
   D. cleanout

49. The size of No. ⑯ is

   A. 2" x 2"
   C. 3" x 3"
   B. 2" x 3"
   D. 4" x 4"

50. No. ⑱ is a

   A. pressure reducing valve
   B. butterfly valve
   C. curb cock
   D. sprinkler head

KEY (CORRECT ANSWERS)

1. C	11. A	21. D	31. A	41. D
2. B	12. C	22. D	32. D	42. A
3. C	13. A	23. B	33. C	43. A
4. D	14. B	24. A	34. A	44. C
5. D	15. C	25. A	35. C	45. B
6. B	16. A	26. B	36. B	46. C
7. B	17. A	27. B	37. D	47. A
8. A	18. D	28. D	38. D	48. B
9. B	19. B	29. D	39. D	49. D
10. D	20. D	30. D	40. B	50. C

EXAMINATION SECTION
TEST 1

DIRECTIONS: Each question or incomplete statement is followed by several suggested answers or completions. Select the one that BEST answers the question or completes the statement. *PRINT THE LETTER OF THE CORRECT ANSWER IN THE SPACE AT THE RIGHT.*

1. Linseed oil putty would MOST likely be used to secure glass in _____ windows. 1._____
   - A. steel casement
   - B. aluminum jalousie
   - C. wood double hung
   - D. aluminum storm

2. Of the following, the one type of glass that should NOT be cut with the ordinary type glass cutter is _____ glass. 2._____
   - A. safety
   - B. plate
   - C. wire
   - D. herculite

3. Thermopane is made of two sheets of glass separated by 3._____
   - A. a sheet of celluloid
   - B. wire mesh
   - C. an air space
   - D. mica

4. Glass is NEVER cut so that it fits snugly inside the frame of a steel casement window. Of the following, the MAIN reason for allowing this space between the glass and the side of the frame is to 4._____
   - A. prevent cracking of the glass in cold weather
   - B. permit the glass to be lined up properly
   - C. allow space for the putty
   - D. eliminate the necessity of polishing the edges of the glass

5. Glass is held in steel sash by means of 5._____
   - A. points
   - B. clips
   - C. plates
   - D. blocks

6. When nailing felt to a roof, the nails should be driven through a 6._____
   - A. tinned disc
   - B. steel washer
   - C. brass plate
   - D. plastic bushing

7. An opening in a parapet wall for draining water from a roof is MOST often called a 7._____
   - A. leader
   - B. gutter
   - C. downspout
   - D. scupper

8. Roofing nails are usually 8._____
   - A. brass
   - B. cement coated
   - C. galvanized
   - D. nickel plated

9. A *street ell* is a fitting having 9._____
   - A. male threads at both ends
   - B. male threads at one end and female threads at the other end
   - C. female threads at both ends
   - D. male threads at one end and a solder connection at the other end

10. Of the following pieces of equipment, the one on which you would MOST likely find a safety (pop-off) valve is a(n)

    A. hot air furnace
    B. air conditioning compressor
    C. hot water heater
    D. dehumidifier

11. Compression fittings are MOST often used with

    A. cast iron bell and spigot pipe
    B. steel flange pipe
    C. copper tubing
    D. transite

12. Water hammer is BEST eliminated by

    A. increasing the size of all the piping
    B. installing an air chamber
    C. replacing the valve seats with neoprene gaskets
    D. flushing the system to remove corrosion

13. The BEST type of pipe to use in a gas line in a domestic installation is

    A. black iron   B. galvanized iron
    C. cast iron   D. wrought steel

14. If there is a pinhole in the float of a toilet tank, the

    A. water will flush continually
    B. toilet cannot flush
    C. tank cannot be filled with water
    D. valve will not shut off so water will overflow into the overflow tube

15. Condensation of moisture in humid weather occurs MOST often on _____ pipe(s).

    A. sewage   B. gas
    C. hot water   D. cold water

16. A gas appliance should be connected to a gas line by means of a(n)

    A. union   B. right and left coupling
    C. elbow   D. close nipple

17. A PRINCIPAL difference between a pipe thread and a machine thread is that the pipe thread is

    A. tapered   B. finer   C. flat   D. longer

18. When joining galvanized iron pipe, pipe joint compound is placed on

    A. the female threads only
    B. the male threads only
    C. both the male and female threads
    D. either the male or the female threads depending on the type of fitting

19. If moisture is trapped between the layers of a 3-ply roof, the heat of a summer day will   19.____

    A. dry the roof out
    B. cause blisters to be formed in the roofing
    C. rot the felt material
    D. have no effect on the roofing

20. Of the following, the metal MOST often used for leaders and gutters is   20.____

    A. monel   B. brass
    C. steel   D. galvanized iron

21. When drilling a small hole in sheet copper, the BEST practice is to   21.____

    A. make a dent with a center punch first
    B. put some cutting oil at the point you intend to drill
    C. use a slow speed drill to prevent overheating
    D. use an auger type bit

22. The reason for annealing sheet copper is to make it   22.____

    A. soft and easier to work
    B. more resistant to weather
    C. easier to solder
    D. harder and more resistant to blows

23. In draw filing,   23.____

    A. only the edge of the file is used
    B. a triangle file is generally used
    C. the file is pulled toward the mechanic's body in filing
    D. the file must have a safe edge

24. The type of paint that uses water as a thinner is   24.____

    A. enamel   B. latex   C. shellac   D. lacquer

25. The reason for placing a 6" sub-base of cinders under a concrete sidewalk is to   25.____

    A. provide flexibility in the surface
    B. permit drainage of water
    C. prevent chemicals in the soil from damaging the sidewalk
    D. allow room for the concrete to expand

26. The BEST material to use to lubricate a door lock is   26.____

    A. penetrating oil   B. pike oil
    C. graphite   D. light grease

27. Assume that the color of the flame from a gas stove is bright yellow.   27.____
    To correct this, you should

    A. close the air flap
    B. open the air flap
    C. increase the gas pressure
    D. increase the size of the gas opening

28. In a 110-220 volt three-wire circuit, the neutral wire is usually

   A. black   B. red   C. white   D. green

29. Brushes on fractional horsepower universal motors are MOST often made of

   A. flexible copper strands   B. rigid carbon blocks
   C. thin wire strips   D. collector rings

30. Leaks from the stem of a faucet can generally be stopped by replacing the

   A. bibb washer   B. seat   C. packing   D. gasket

31. Of the following, the BEST procedure to follow with a frozen water pipe is to

   A. allow the pipe to thaw out by itself as the weather gets warmer
   B. put anti-freeze into the pipe above the section that is frozen
   C. turn on the hot water heater
   D. open the faucet closest to the frozen pipe and warm the pipe with a blow torch, starting at this point

32. The one of the following that is NOT usually changed by a central air conditioning system is the

   A. volume of air in the system   B. humidity of the air
   C. dust in the air   D. air pressure of the system

33. The temperature of a domestic hot water system is MOST often controlled by a(n)

   A. relief valve   B. aquastat   C. barometer   D. thermostat

34. Draft in a chimney is MOST often controlled by a(n)

   A. damper   B. gate
   C. orifice   D. cross connection

35. Assume that a refrigerator motor operates continuously for excessively long periods of time.
    The FIRST item you should check to locate the defect is the

   A. plug in the outlet
   B. door gasket
   C. direction of rotation of the motor
   D. motor switch

36. Assume that after replacing a defective motor for a large electric fan, you find that the fan is rotating in the wrong direction.
    If the motor is a split phase motor, with the shaft at one end only, the trouble could be CORRECTED by

   A. reversing the fan on its shaft
   B. turning the motor end for end
   C. interchanging the connections on the field terminals of the motor
   D. reversing the plug in the electric outlet

37. In order to properly hang a door, shims are frequently inserted under the hinges. These shims are MOST often made of

   A. cardboard
   B. sheet steel
   C. bakelite
   D. the same materials as the hinges

38. Flooring nails are usually _____ nails.

   A. casing   B. common   C. cut   D. clinch

39. Over a doorway, to support brick, you will usually find

   A. steel angles   B. hanger bolts
   C. wooden headers   D. stirrups

40. Insulation of steam pipes is MOST often done with

   A. asbestos   B. celotex   C. alundum   D. sheathing

41. Assume that only the first few coils of a hot water convector used for heating a room are hot.
    To correct this, you should FIRST

   A. increase the water pressure
   B. increase the water temperature
   C. bleed the air out of the convector
   D. clean the convector pipes

42. The MAIN reason for grounding the outer sheel of an electric fixture is to

   A. provide additional support for the fixture
   B. reduce the cost of installation of the fixture
   C. provide a terminal to which the wires can be attached
   D. reduce the chance of electric shock

43. In woodwork, countersinking is MOST often done for

   A. lag screws   B. carriage bolts
   C. hanger bolts   D. flat head screws

44. Bridging is MOST often used in connection with

   A. door frames   B. window openings
   C. floor joists   D. stud walls

45. A saddle is part of a

   A. doorway   B. window
   C. stair well   D. bulkhead

46. To make it easier to drive screws into hard wood, it is BEST to

    A. use a screwdriver that is longer than that used for soft wood
    B. rub the threads of the screw on a bar of soap
    C. oil the screw threads
    D. use a square shank screwdriver assisted by a wrench

47. In using a doweled joint to make a repair of a wooden door, it is important to remember that the dowel

    A. hole must be smaller in diameter than the dowel so that there is a tight fit
    B. hole must be longer than the dowel to provide a room for excess glue
    C. must be of the same type of wood as the door frame
    D. must be held in place by a small screw while waiting for the glue to set

48. The edges of MOST finished wood flooring are

    A. tongue and groove   B. mortise and tenon
    C. bevel and miter   D. lap and scarf

49. For the SMOOTHEST finish, sanding of wood should be done

    A. in a circular direction
    B. diagonally against the grain
    C. across the grain
    D. parallel with the grain

50. To prevent splintering of wood when boring a hole through it, the BEST practice is to

    A. drill at a slow speed
    B. use a scrap piece to back up the work
    C. use an auger bit
    D. ease up the pressure on the drill when the drill is almost through the wood

KEY (CORRECT ANSWERS)

1. C	11. C	21. A	31. D	41. C
2. D	12. B	22. A	32. D	42. D
3. C	13. A	23. C	33. B	43. D
4. A	14. D	24. B	34. A	44. C
5. B	15. D	25. B	35. B	45. A
6. A	16. B	26. C	36. C	46. B
7. D	17. A	27. B	37. A	47. B
8. C	18. B	28. C	38. C	48. A
9. B	19. B	29. B	39. A	49. D
10. C	20. D	30. C	40. A	50. B

TEST 2

DIRECTIONS: Each question or incomplete statement is followed by several suggested answers or completions. Select the one that BEST answers the question or completes the statement. *PRINT THE LETTER OF THE CORRECT ANSWER IN THE SPACE AT THE RIGHT.*

1. A *speed nut* has   1.____
    A. no threads
    B. threads that are coarser than a standard nut
    C. threads that are finer than s standard nut
    D. fewer threads than a standard nut

2. The BEST tool to use to remove the burr and sharp edge resulting from cutting tubing with a tube cutter is a   2.____
    A. file   B. scraper   C. reamer   D. knife

3. A router is used PRINCIPALLY to   3.____
    A. clean pipe   B. cut grooves in wood
    C. bend electric conduit   D. sharpen tools

4. The principle of operation of a sabre saw is MOST similar to that of a _____ saw.   4.____
    A. circular   B. radial   C. swing   D. jig

5. A full thread cutting set would have both taps and   5.____
    A. cutters   B. bushings   C. dies   D. plugs

6. The proper flux to use for soldering electric wire connections is   6.____
    A. rosin   B. killed acid
    C. borax   D. zinc chloride

7. A fusestat differs from an ordinary plug fuse in that a fusestat has   7.____
    A. less current carrying capacity
    B. different size threads
    C. an aluminum shell instead of a copper shell
    D. no threads

8. A grounding type 120-volt receptacle differs from an ordinary electric receptacle MAINLY in that a grounding receptacle   8.____
    A. is larger than the ordinary receptacle
    B. has openings for a three prong plug
    C. can be used for larger machinery
    D. has a built-in circuit breaker

9. A carbide tip is MOST often found on a bit used for drilling   9.____
    A. concrete   B. wood   C. steel   D. brass

10. The MAIN reason for using oil on an oilstone is to

    A. make the surface of the stone smoother
    B. prevent clogging of the pores of the stone
    C. reduce the number of times the stone has to be *dressed*
    D. prevent gouging of the stone's surface

11. The sum of the following numbers, 1 3/4, 3 1/6, 5 1/2, 6 5/8, and 9 1/4, is

    A. 26 1/8   B. 26 1/4   C. 26 1/2   D. 26 3/4

12. If a piece of plywood measures 5' 1 1/4" x 3' 2 1/2", the number of square feet in this board is MOST NEARLY

    A. 15.8   B. 16.1   C. 16.4   D. 16.7

13. Assume that in quantity purchases the city receives a discount of 33 1/3%.
    If a one gallon can of paint retails at $5.33 per gallon, the cost of 375 gallons of this paint is MOST NEARLY

    A. $1,332.50   B. $1,332.75   C. $1,333.00   D. $1,333.25

14. Assume that eight barrels of cement together weigh a total of 3004 lbs. and 12 oz.
    If there are four bags of cement per barrel, then the weight of one bag of cement is MOST NEARLY _____ lbs.

    A. 93.1   B. 93.5   C. 93.9   D. 94.3

15. Assume that one man cuts 50 nameplates per hour, whereas his co-worker cuts 55 nameplates per hour.
    At the end of 7 hours, the first man will have cut fewer nameplates than the second man by

    A. 9.3%   B. 9.5%   C. 9.7%   D. 9.9%

16. Under the same conditions, the one of the following that dries the FASTEST is

    A. shellac   B. varnish   C. enamel   D. lacquer

17. Interior wood trim in a building is MOST often made of

    A. hemlock   B. pine   C. cedar   D. oak

18. Gaskets are seldom made of

    A. rubber   B. lead   C. asbestos   D. vinyl

19. Toggle bolts are MOST frequently used to

    A. fasten shelf supports to a hollow block wall
    B. fasten furniture legs to table tops
    C. anchor machinery to a concrete floor
    D. join two pieces of sheet metal

20. Rubber will deteriorate FASTEST when it is constantly in contact with

    A. air   B. water   C. oil   D. soapsuds

21. Stoppage of water flow is often caused by dirt <u>accumulating</u> in an elbow. 21._____
    As used in the above sentence, the word <u>accumulating</u> means MOST NEARLY

    A. clogging   B. collecting   C. rusting   D. confined

22. The surface of the metal was <u>embossed</u>. 22._____
    As used in the above sentence, the word <u>embossed</u> means MOST NEARLY

    A. polished   B. rough   C. raised   D. painted

Questions 23-24.

DIRECTIONS: Questions 23 and 24 are to be answered in accordance with the following paragraph.

When fixing an upper sash cord, you must also remove the lower sash. To do this, the parting strip between the sash must be removed. Now remove the cover from the weight box channel, cut off the cord as before, and pull it over the pulleys. Pull your new cord over the pulleys and down into the channel, where it may be fastened to the weight. The cord for an upper sash is cut off 1" or 2" below the pulley with the weight resting on the floor of the pocket and the cord held taut. These measurements allow for slight stretching of the cord. When the cord is cut to length, it can be pulled up over the pulley and tied with a single common knot in the end to fit into the socket in the sash groove. If the knot protrudes beyond the face of the sash, tap it gently to flatten. In this way, it will not become frayed from constant rubbing against the groove.

23. When repairing the upper sash cord, the FIRST thing to do is to 23._____

    A. remove the lower sash
    B. cut the existing sash cord
    C. remove the parting strip
    D. measure the length of new cord necessary

24. According to the above paragraph, the rope may become frayed if the 24._____

    A. pulley is too small   B. knot sticks out
    C. cord is too long   D. weight is too heavy

25. In the repair of the sash cord mentioned in the paragraph for Questions 23 and 24, the 25._____
    MAIN reason for cutting off the sash cord below the bottom of the pulley is to

    A. prevent the cord from tangling
    B. save on amount of cord used
    C. prevent the sash weight from hitting the bottom of the frame in use
    D. provide room for tying the knot

26. Of the following drawings, the one that would be considered an *elevation* of a building is the 26._____

    A. floor plan   B. front view   C. cross section   D. site plan

27. On a plan, the symbol shown at the right USUALLY represents a(n) 27._____

    A. duplex receptacle   B. electric switch
    C. ceiling outlet   D. pull box

28. On a plan, the symbol _____ - _____ - USUALLY represents a

    A. center line B. hidden outline
    C. long break D. dimension line

29. Assume that on a plan you see the following: 1/4" - 20 NC-2. This refers to the

    A. diameter of a hole
    B. size and type of screw thread
    C. taper of a pin
    D. scale at which the plan is drawn

30.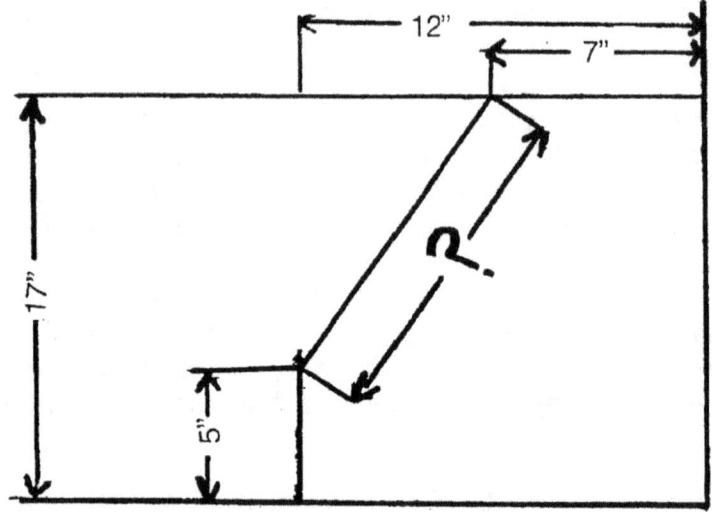

    In reference to the above sketch, the length of the diagonal part of the plate indicated by the question mark is MOST NEARLY

    A. 13"   B. 14"   C. 15"   D. 16"

31. To increase the workability of concrete without changing its strength, the BEST procedure to follow is to increase the percentage of

    A. water B. cement and sand
    C. cement and water D. water and sand

32. The MAIN reason for covering freshly poured concrete with tar paper is to

    A. prevent evaporation of water
    B. stop people from walking on the concrete
    C. protect the concrete from rain
    D. keep back any earth that may fall on the concrete

33. The MAIN reason for using air-entrained cement in sidewalks is to

    A. protect the concrete from the effects of freezing
    B. color the concrete
    C. speed up the setting time of the concrete
    D. make the concrete more workable

34. Assume that a reinforcing bar used for concrete is badly rusted. Before using this bar,

    A. it is not necessary to remove any rust
    B. only loose rust need be removed
    C. all rust should be removed
    D. all rust should be removed and a coat of red lead paint is applied

34.____

35. Assume that freshly poured concrete has been exposed to freezing temperatures for 6 hours.
    In all likelihood, this concrete

    A. has been permanently damaged
    B. will harden properly as soon as the air temperature warms up
    C. will harden properly even though the temperature remains below freezing
    D. will eventually harden properly, but it will take much longer than usual

35.____

36. Assume that concrete for a floor in a play yard is to be placed directly on the earth. On checking, you find that, because of a recent rain, the earth is damp.
    You should

    A. wait till the sun dries the earth before placing the concrete
    B. use a waterproofing material between the concrete slab and the earth
    C. use less water in the concrete mix
    D. ignore the damp earth and place the concrete as you normally would

36.____

37. The MAJOR disadvantage of *floating* the surface of concrete too much is that the

    A. surface will become too rough
    B. surface will become weak and will wear rapidly
    C. initial set will be disturbed
    D. concrete cannot be cured properly

37.____

38. In addition to water and sand, mortar mix for a cinder block wall is usually made of

    A. gravel and lime   B. plaster and cement
    C. gravel and cement   D. lime and cement

38.____

39. The *nominal* size of a standard cinder block is

    A. 8" x 6" x 16"   B. 8" x 8" x 16"
    C. 8" x 12" x 12"   D. 6" x 8" x 12"

39.____

40. The *bond* of a brick wall refers to the

    A. arrangement of headers and stretchers
    B. time it takes for the mortar to set
    C. way a brick wall is tied in to an intersecting wall
    D. type of mortar used in the wall

40.____

41. The purpose of *tooling* when erecting a brick wall is to

    A. cut the brick to fit into a small space
    B. insure that the brick is laid level
    C. compact the mortar at the joints
    D. hold the brick in place till the mortar sets

41.____

42. Mortar is BEST cleaned off the face of a brick wall by using

    A. muriatic acid
    B. lye
    C. oxalic acid
    D. sodium hypochlorite

43. A brick wall is *pointed* to

    A. make sure it is the correct height
    B. repair the mortar joints
    C. set the brick in place
    D. arrange the mortar bed before setting the brick

44. The second coat in a three-coat plaster job is the _____ coat.

    A. scratch   B. brown   C. putty   D. lime

45. To repair fine cracks in a plastered wall, the PROPER material to use is

    A. lime
    B. cement wash
    C. perlite
    D. spackle

46. Gypsum lath for plastering is purchased in

    A. strips 5/16" x 1 1/2" x 4'
    B. rolls 3/8" x 48" x 96"
    C. boards 1/2" x 16" x 48"
    D. sheets 5/16" x 27" x 96"

47. The PRINCIPAL reason for using acoustic tile instead of ordinary tile is that the acoustic tile

    A. deadens sound
    B. is easier to apply
    C. is longer lasting
    D. costs less

48. The MAXIMUM thickness of the finish coat of white plaster is MOST NEARLY

    A. 1/8"   B. 1/4"   C. 3/8"   D. 1/2"

49. When using tape to conceal joints in dry wall construction, the FIRST operation is

    A. channelling the grooves between boards
    B. applying cement to the joints
    C. sanding the edges of the joints
    D. packing the tape into the joints

50. For the FIRST coat of plaster on wire lath, plaster of paris is mixed with

    A. cement   B. sand   C. lime   D. mortar

KEY (CORRECT ANSWERS)

1. A	11. B	21. B	31. C	41. C
2. C	12. C	22. C	32. A	42. A
3. B	13. A	23. C	33. A	43. B
4. D	14. C	24. B	34. B	44. B
5. C	15. D	25. C	35. A	45. D
6. A	16. D	26. B	36. D	46. C
7. B	17. B	27. C	37. B	47. A
8. B	18. D	28. A	38. D	48. A
9. A	19. A	29. B	39. B	49. B
10. B	20. C	30. A	40. A	50. B

EXAMINATION SECTION
TEST 1

DIRECTIONS: Each question or incomplete statement is followed by several suggested answers or completions. Select the one that BEST answers the question or completes the statement. *PRINT THE LETTER OF THE CORRECT ANSWER IN THE SPACE AT THE RIGHT.*

1.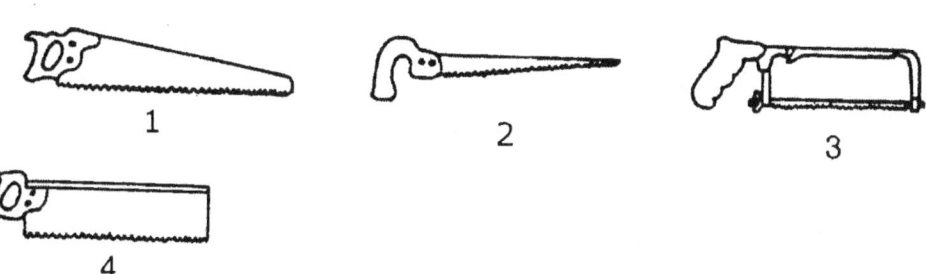

    The saw that is used PRINCIPALLY where curved cuts are to be made is numbered

    A. 1   B. 2   C. 3   D. 4

2.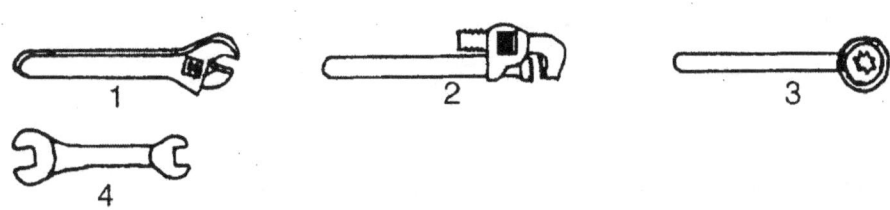

    The wrench that is used PRINCIPALLY for pipe work is numbered

    A. 1   B. 2   C. 3   D. 4

3.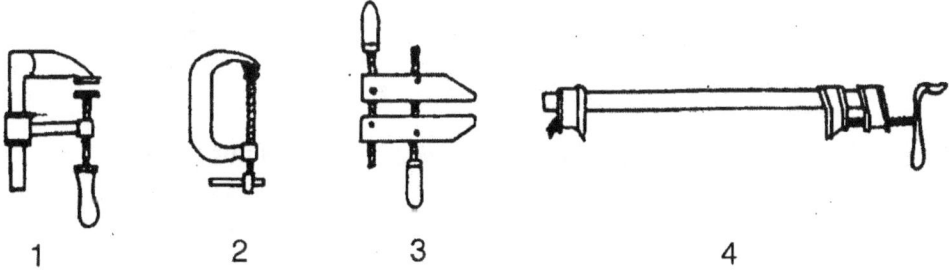

    The carpenter's *hand screw* is numbered

    A. 1   B. 2   C. 3   D. 4

4.

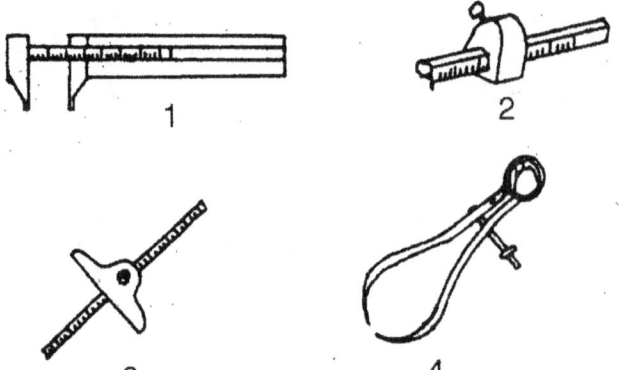

The tool used to measure the depth of a hole is numbered

A. 1   B. 2   C. 3   D. 4

5.

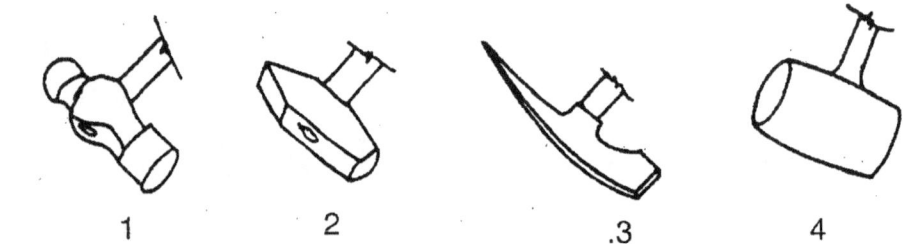

The tool that is BEST suited for use with a wood chisel is numbered

A. 1   B. 2   C. 3   D. 4

6.

The screw head that would be tightened with an *Allen* wrench is numbered

A. 1   B. 2   C. 3   D. 4

7.

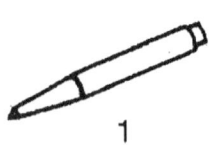   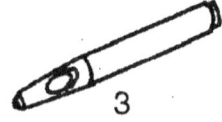

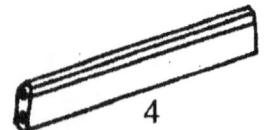

The center punch is numbered

A. 1   B. 2   C. 3   D. 4

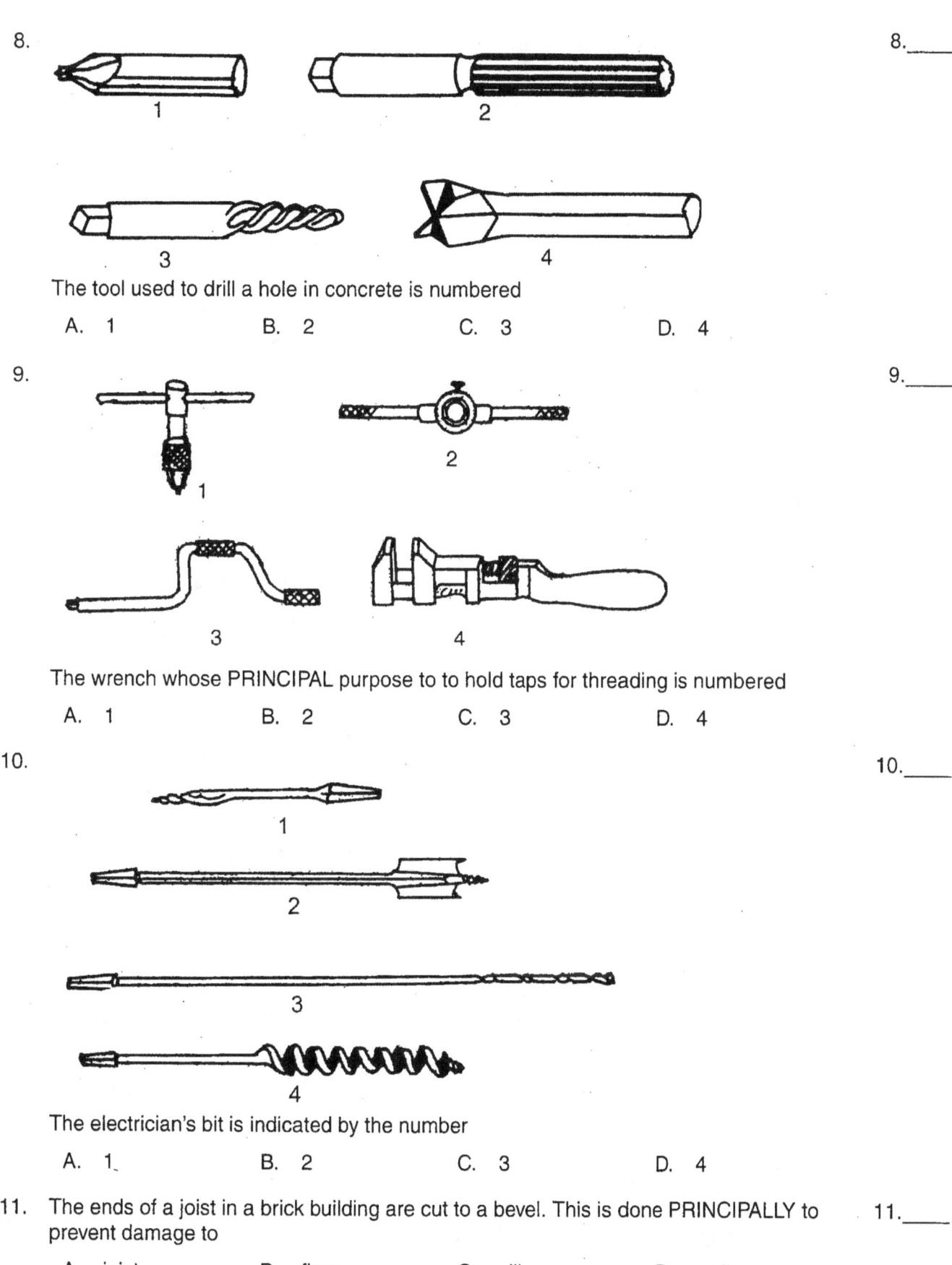

8. The tool used to drill a hole in concrete is numbered

   A. 1   B. 2   C. 3   D. 4

9. The wrench whose PRINCIPAL purpose to to hold taps for threading is numbered

   A. 1   B. 2   C. 3   D. 4

10. The electrician's bit is indicated by the number

    A. 1   B. 2   C. 3   D. 4

11. The ends of a joist in a brick building are cut to a bevel. This is done PRINCIPALLY to prevent damage to

    A. joist   B. floor   C. sill   D. wall

12. Of the following, the wood that is MOST commonly used today for floor joists is 12.____

    A. long leaf yellow pine B. douglas fir
    C. oak D. birch

13. Quarter-sawed lumber is preferred for the BEST finished flooring PRINCIPALLY because it 13.____

    A. has the greatest strength B. shrinks the least
    C. is the easiest to nail D. is the easiest to handle

14. A tool used in hanging doors is a 14.____

    A. miter gauge B. line level
    C. try square D. butt gauge

15. Of the following, the MAXIMUM height that would be considered acceptable for a stair riser is 15.____

    A. 6 1/2" B. 7 1/2" C. 8 1/2" D. 9 1/2"

16. The PRINCIPAL reason for *cross banding* the layers of wood in a plywood panel is to _____ of the panel. 16.____

    A. reduce warping B. increase the strength
    C. reduce the cost D. increase the beauty

17. The part of a tree that will produce the DENSEST wood is the _____ wood. 17.____

    A. spring B. summer C. sap D. heart

18. Casing nails MOST NEARLY resemble _____ nails. 18.____

    A. common B. roofing C. form D. finishing

19. Lumber in quantity is ordered by 19.____

    A. cubic feet B. foot board measure
    C. lineal feet D. weight and length

20. For finishing of wood, BEST results are obtained by sanding 20.____

    A. with a circular motion
    B. against the grain
    C. with the grain
    D. with a circular motion on edges and against the grain on the flat parts

21. A *chase* in a brick wall is a 21.____

    A. pilaster B. waterstop C. recess D. corbel

22. Parging refers to 22.____

    A. increasing the thickness of a brick wall
    B. plastering the back of face brickwork
    C. bonding face brick to backing blocks
    D. leveling each course of brick

23. The PRINCIPAL reason for requiring brick to be wetted before laying is that

   A. less water is required in the mortar
   B. efflorescence is prevented
   C. the brick will not absorb as much water from the mortar
   D. cool brick is easier to handle

24. In brickwork, muriatic acid is commonly used to

   A. increase the strength of the mortar
   B. etch the brick
   C. waterproof the wall
   D. clean the wall

25. Cement mortar can be made easier to work by the addition of a small quantity of

   A. lime   B. soda   C. litharge   D. plaster

26. Headers in brickwork are used to _____ the wall.

   A. strengthen   B. reduce the cost of
   C. speed the erection of   D. align

27. Joints in brick walls are tooled

   A. immediately after each brick is laid
   B. after the mortar has had its initial set
   C. after the entire wall is completed
   D. 28 days after the wall has been built

28. If cement mortar has begun to set before it can be used in a wall, the BEST thing to do is to

   A. use the mortar immediately as is
   B. add a small quantity of lime
   C. add some water and mix thoroughly
   D. discard the mortar

29. A *bat* in brickwork is a

   A. brace to hold a wall temporarily in place
   B. stick used to aid in mixing of mortar
   C. broken piece of brick used to fill short spaces
   D. curved brick used in ornamental work

30. The proportions by volume of cement, lime, and sand in a cement-lime mortar should be, according to the Building Code,

   A. 1:1:3   B. 2:1:6   C. 1:1:6   D. 1:2:6

31. The BEST flux to use when soldering galvanized iron is

   A. killed acid   B. sal-ammoniac
   C. muriatic acid   D. resin

32. When soldering a vertical joint, the soldering iron should be tinned on _____ side(s).

    A. 1   B. 2   C. 3   D. 4

33. The difference between *right hand* and *left hand* tin snips is the

    A. relative position of the cutting jaws
    B. shape of the cutting jaws
    C. shape of the handles
    D. relative position of the handles

34. A machine used to bend sheet metal is called a

    A. router   B. planer   C. brake   D. swage

35. The type of solder that would be used in *hard soldering* would be _____ solder.

    A. bismuth   B. wiping   C. 50-50   D. silver

36. Roll roofing material is usually felt which has been impregnated with

    A. cement   B. mastic   C. tar   D. latex

37. The purpose of flashing on roofs is to

    A. secure roofing materials to the roof
    B. make it easier to lay the roofing
    C. prevent leaks through the roof
    D. insulate the roof from excessive heat

38. The tool used to spread hot pitch on a three-ply roofing job is a

    A. mop   B. spreader   C. pusher   D. broom

39. The cutting of glass can be facilitated by dipping the cutting wheel in

    A. *3-in-1* oil   B. water   C. lard   D. kerosene

40. The strips of metal used to hold glass to the window frame while it is being puttied are called

    A. hold-downs   B. points   C. wedges   D. triangles

41. The type of chain used with sash weights is _____ link.

    A. flat   B. round
    C. figure-eight   D. basket-weave

42. The material that would be used to seal around a window frame is

    A. oakum   B. litharge   C. grout   D. calking

43. The function of a window sill is MOST NEARLY the same as that of a

    A. jamb   B. coping   C. lintel   D. brick

44. Lightweight plaster would be made with

    A. sand   B. cinders   C. potash   D. vermiculite

45. The FIRST coat of plaster to be applied on a three-coat plaster job is the _____ coat. 45._____

    A. brown B. scratch C. white D. keene

46. Screeds in plaster work are used to 46._____

    A. remove larger sizes of sand
    B. hold the batch of plaster before it is applied
    C. apply the plaster to the wall
    D. guide the plasterer in making, an even wall

47. The FIRST coat of plaster over rock lath should be a _____ plaster. 47._____

    A. gypsum B. lime
    C. portland cement D. puzzolan cement

48. In plastering, a *hawk* is used to _____ plaster. 48._____

    A. apply B. hold C. scratch D. smooth

49. When mixing concrete by hand, the order in which the ingredients should be mixed is: 49._____

    A. water, cement, sand, stone
    B. sand, cement, water, stone
    C. stone, water, sand, cement
    D. stone, sand, cement, water

50. The PRINCIPAL reason for covering a concrete sidewalk with straw or paper after the concrete has been poured is to 50._____

    A. prevent people from walking on the concrete while it is still wet
    B. impart a rough non-slip surface to the concrete
    C. prevent excessive evaporation of water in the concrete
    D. shorten the length of time it would take for the concrete to harden

KEY (CORRECT ANSWERS)

1. B	11. D	21. C	31. C	41. A
2. B	12. B	22. B	32. A	42. D
3. C	13. B	23. C	33. A	43. B
4. C	14. D	24. D	34. C	44. D
5. D	15. B	25. A	35. D	45. B
6. C	16. A	26. A	36. C	46. D
7. A	17. D	27. B	37. C	47. A
8. D	18. D	28. D	38. A	48. B
9. A	19. B	29. C	39. D	49. D
10. C	20. C	30. C	40. B	50. C

TEST 2

DIRECTIONS: Each question or incomplete statement is followed by several suggested answers or completions. Select the one that BEST answers the question or completes the statement. *PRINT THE LETTER OF THE CORRECT ANSWER IN THE SPACE AT THE RIGHT.*

1. When colored concrete is required, the colors used should be   1._____

    A. colors in oil
    B. mineral pigments
    C. tempera colors
    D. water colors

2. Concrete is *rubbed* with a(n)   2._____

    A. emery wheel
    B. carborundum brick
    C. sandstone
    D. alundum stick

3. To prevent concrete from sticking to forms, the forms should be painted with   3._____

    A. oil   B. kerosene   C. water   D. lime

4. The reinforcement in a concrete floor slab is referred to as 6"-6" x #6-#6. The type of reinforcing that is being used is   4._____

    A. steel bars
    B. wire mesh
    C. angle irons
    D. grating plate

5. One method of measuring the consistency of a concrete mix is by means of a _____ test.   5._____

    A. penetration   B. flow   C. slump   D. weight

6. A chemical that is sometimes used to prevent the freezing of concrete in cold weather is   6._____

    A. alum
    B. glycerine
    C. calcium chloride
    D. sodium nitrate

7. The one of the following that is LEAST commonly used for columns is   7._____

    A. wide flange beams
    B. angles
    C. concrete-filled pipe
    D. *I* beams

8. Fire protection of steel floor beams is MOST frequently accomplished by the use of   8._____

    A. gypsum block
    B. brick
    C. rock wool fill
    D. vermiculite gypsum plaster

9. A *Pittsburgh lock* is a(n)   9._____

    A. emergency door lock
    B. sheet metal joint
    C. elevator safety
    D. boiler valve

10. In order to drill a hole at right angle to the horizontal axis of a round bar, the bar should be held in a   10._____

    A. step block
    B. C-block
    C. hand pliers
    D. V-block

30

11. The procedure to follow in the lubrication of maintenance shop equipment is to lubricate   11._____

    A. when you can spare the time
    B. only when necessary
    C. at regular intervals
    D. when the equipment is in operation

12. Of the following items, the one which is NOT used in making fastenings to masonry or   12._____
    plaster walls is a(n)

    A. lead shield   B. expansion bolt
    C. rawl plug   D. steel bushing

13. When a common straight ladder is used to paint a wall, the safe distance that the foot of   13._____
    the ladder should be set away from the wall is MOST NEARLY _____ the length of the
    ladder.

    A. one-eighth   B. one-quarter
    C. one-half   D. five-eighths

14. The term *bell and spigot* usually refers to   14._____

    A. refrigerator motors   B. cast iron pipes
    C. steam radiator outlets   D. electrical receptacles

15. In plumbing work, a valve which allows water to flow in one direction only is commonly   15._____
    known as a _____ valve.

    A. check   B. globe   C. gate   D. stop

16. A pipe coupling is BEST used to connect two pieces of pipe of   16._____

    A. the same diameter in a straight line
    B. the same diameter at right angles to each other
    C. different diameters at a 45° angle
    D. different diameters at an 1/8th bend

17. A fitting or pipe with many outlets relatively close together is commonly called a   17._____

    A. manifold   B. gooseneck
    C. flange union   D. return bend

18. To locate the center in the end of a sound shaft, the BEST tool to use is a(n)   18._____

    A. ruler   B. divider
    C. hermaphrodite caliper   D. micrometer

19. When cutting a piece of 1 1/4" O.D. 20 gauge brass tubing with a hand hacksaw, it is   19._____
    BEST to use a blade having _____ teeth per inch.

    A. 14   B. 18   C. 22   D. 32

20. When cutting a piece of 1" O.D. extra-heavy pipe with a pipe cutter, a burr usually forms   20._____
    on the inside and the outside of the pipe. These burrs are BEST removed by means of a
    pipe

    A. tap and a file   B. wrench and rough stone
    C. reamer and a file   D. drill and a chisel

21. Artificial respiration should be started immediately on a man who has suffered an electric shock if he is

   A. *unconscious* and breathing
   B. *unconscious* and not breathing
   C. *conscious* and in a daze
   D. *conscious* and badly burned

22. The fuse of a certain circuit has blown and is replaced with a fuse of the same rating which also blows when the switch is closed.
In this case,

   A. a fuse of higher current rating should be used
   B. a fuse of higher voltage rating should be used
   C. the fuse should be temporarily replaced by a heavy piece of wire
   D. the circuit should be checked

23. Operating an incandescent electric light bulb at less than its rated voltage will result in

   A. shorter life and brighter light
   B. longer life and dimmer light
   C. brighter light and longer life
   D. dimmer light and shorter life

24. In order to control a lamp from two different positions, it is necessary to use

   A. two single pole switches
   B. one single pole switch and one four-way switch
   C. two three-way switches
   D. one single pole switch and one four-way switch

25.

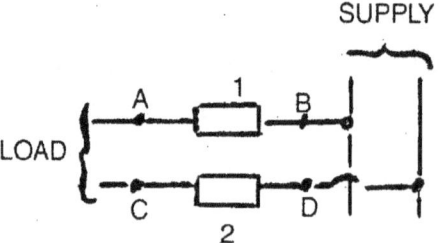

One method of testing fuses is to connect a pair of test lamps in the circuit in such a manner that the test lamp will light up if the fuse is good and will remain dark if the fuse is bad. In the above illustration 1 and 2 are fuses.
In order to test if fuse 1 is bad, test lamps should be connected between

   A. A and B   B. B and D   C. A and D   D. C and B

26. The PRINCIPAL reason for the grounding of electrical equipment and circuits is to

   A. prevent short circuits   B. insure safety from shock
   C. save power   D. increase voltage

27. The ordinary single-pole flush wall type switch must be connected

    A. across the line
    B. in the *hot* conductor
    C. in the grounded conductor
    D. in the white conductor

28. A D.C. shunt motor runs in the wrong direction. This fault can be CORRECTED by

    A. reversing the connections of both the field and the armature
    B. interchanging the connections of either main or auxiliar windings
    C. interchanging the connections to either the field or the armature windings
    D. interchanging the connections to the line of the power leads

29. The MOST common type of motor that can be used with both A.C. and D.C. sources is the _____ motor.

    A. compound   B. repulsion   C. series   D. shunt

30. A fluorescent fixture in a new building has been in use for several months without trouble. Recently, the ends of the fluorscent lamp have remained lighted when the light was switched off.
    The BEST way to clear up this trouble is to replace the

    A. lamp   B. ballast   C. starter   D. sockets

31. The BEST wood to use for handles of tools such as axes and hammers is

    A. hemlock   B. pine   C. oak   D. hickory

32. A *hanger bolt*

    A. has a square head
    B. is bent in a *U* shape
    C. has a different type of thread at each end
    D. is threaded the entire length from point to head

33. A stone frequently used to sharpen tools is

    A. carborundum   B. bauxite   C. resin   D. slate

34. A strike plate is MOST closely associated with a

    A. lock   B. sash   C. butt   D. tie rod

35. The material that distinguishes a terrazzo floor from an ordinary concrete floor is

    A. cinders
    B. marble chip
    C. cut stone
    D. non-slip aggregate

36. A room is 7'6" wide by 9'0" long with a ceiling height of 8'0". One gallon of flat paint will cover approximately 400 square feet of wall.
    The number of gallons of this paint required to paint the walls of this room, making no deductions for windows or doors, is MOST NEARLY _____ gallon.

    A. 1/4   B. 1/2   C. 3/4   D. 1

37. The cost of a certain job is broken down as follows:
    Materials $375
    Rental of equipment 120
    Labor   315
    The percentage of the total cost of the job that can be charged to materials is MOST NEARLY

    A. 40%   B. 42%   C. 44%   D. 46%

38. By trial, it is found that by using two cubic feet of sand, a five cubic foot batch of concrete is produced.
    Using the same proportions, the amount of sand required to produce 2 cubic yards of concrete is MOST NEARLY _____ cu.ft.

    A. 20   B. 22   C. 24   D. 26

39. It takes 4 men 6 days to do a certain job.
    Working at the same speed, the number of days it will take 3 men to do this job is

    A. 7   B. 8   C. 9   D. 10

40. The cost of rawl plugs is $2.75 per gross. The cost of 2,448 rawl plugs is

    A. $46.75   B. $47.25   C. $47.75   D. $48.25

41. *Rigidity of the hammer handle enables the operator to control and direct the force of the blow.*
    As used above, *rigidity* means MOST NEARLY

    A. straightness   B. strength
    C. shape   D. stiffness

42. *For precision work, center punches are ground to a fine tapered point.* As used above, *tapered* means MOST NEARLY

    A. conical   B. straight   C. accurate   D. smooth

43. *There are limitations to the drilling of metals by hand power.*
    As used above, *limitations* means MOST NEARLY

    A. advantages   B. restrictions
    C. difficulties   D. benefits

Questions 44-45.

DIRECTIONS: Questions 44 and 45 are based on the following paragraph.

Because electric drills run at high speed, the cutting edges of a twist drill are heated quickly. If the metal is thick, the drill point must be withdrawn from the hole frequently to cool it and clear out chips. Forcing the drill continuously into a deep hole will heat it, thereby spoiling its temper and cutting edges. A portable electric drill has the advantage that it can be taken to the work and used to drill holes in material too large to handle in a drill press.

44. According to the above paragraph, overheating of a twist drill will

    A. slow down the work   B. cause excessive drill breakage
    C. dull the drill   D. spoil the accuracy of the work

45. According to the above paragraph, one method of preventing overheating of a twist drill is to 45.____

    A. use cooling oil
    B. drill a smaller pilot hole first
    C. use a drill press
    D. remove the drill from the work frequently

Questions 46-50.

DIRECTIONS: Questions 46 to 50 are to be answered in accordance with the sketch shown below.

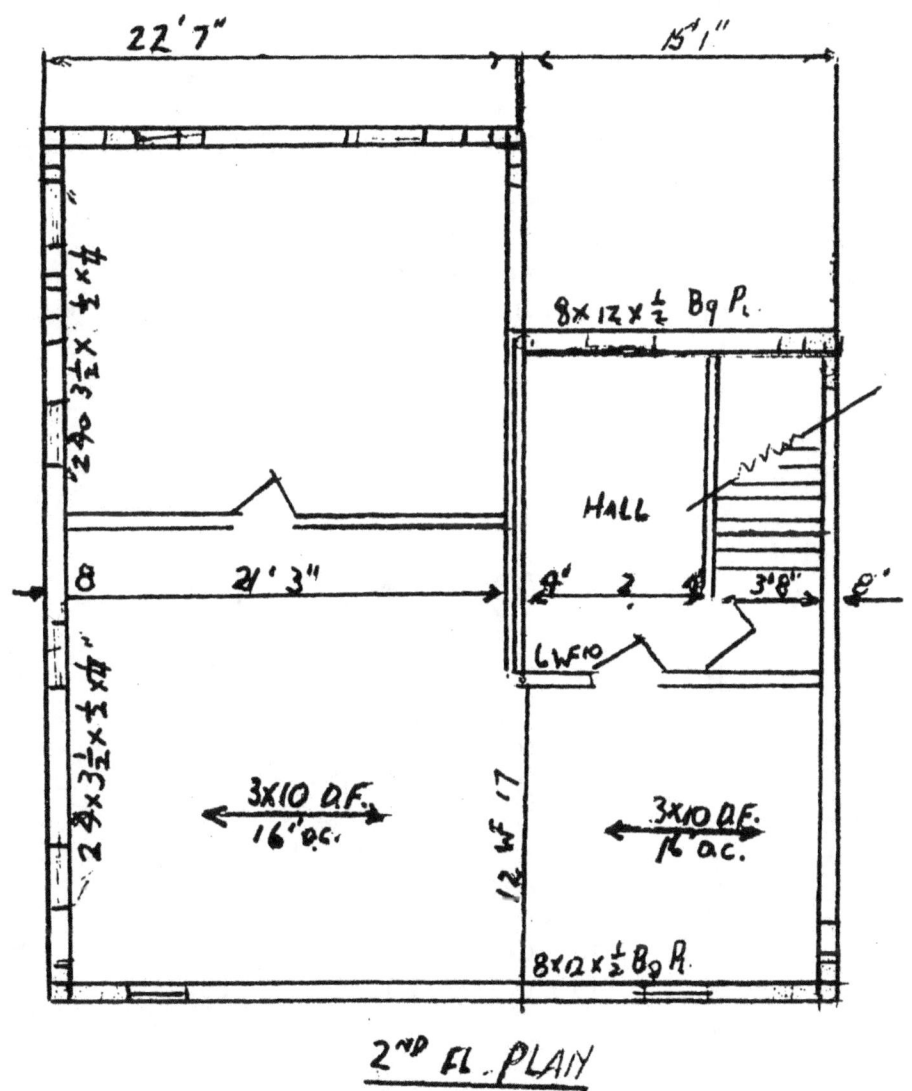

46. The one of the following statements that is CORRECT is the building 46.____

    A. is of fireproof construction
    B. has masonry walls with wood joists
    C. is of wood frame construction
    D. has timber joists and girders

47. The one of the following statements that is CORRECT is 47.____

    A. the stairway from the ground continues through the roof
    B. there are two means of egress from the second floor of this building
    C. the door on the second floor stair landing opens in the direction of egress
    D. the entire stair is shown on this plan

48. The width of the hall is 48.____

    A. 10'3" B. 10'5" C. 10'7" D. 10'9"

49. The lintels shown are 49.____

    A. angles
    C. an I-beam
    B. a channel and an angle
    D. precast concrete

50. The one of the following statements that is CORRECT is that the steel beam is 50.____

    A. supported by columns at the center and at the ends
    B. entirely supported by the walls
    C. supported on columns at the ends only
    D. supported at the center by a column and at the ends by the walls

KEY (CORRECT ANSWERS)

1. B	11. C	21. B	31. D	41. D
2. B	12. D	22. D	32. C	42. A
3. A	13. B	23. B	33. A	43. B
4. B	14. B	24. C	34. A	44. C
5. C	15. A	25. C	35. B	45. D
6. C	16. A	26. B	36. C	46. B
7. B	17. A	27. B	37. D	47. C
8. D	18. C	28. C	38. B	48. D
9. B	19. D	29. C	39. B	49. A
10. D	20. C	30. C	40. A	50. D

EXAMINATION SECTION
TEST 1

DIRECTIONS: Each question consists of a statement. You are to indicate whether the statement is TRUE (T) or FALSE (F). *PRINT THE LETTER OF THE CORRECT ANSWER IN THE SPACE AT THE RIGHT.*

1. One square foot is equal to 144 square inches.   1.____

2. One cubic foot of water weighs APPROXIMATELY 8 1/2 pounds.   2.____

3. One bag of portland cement weighs APPROXIMATELY 94 pounds.   3.____

4. If a board foot is 12 inches by 12 inches by one inch, the number of board feet in a plank 18 feet long, 10 inches wide, 4 inches thick is 360.   4.____

5. If a cubic foot of water contains 7 1/2 gallons, the number of gallons contained in a tank 6 feet long, 4 feet wide, and 2 feet deep is 360.   5.____

6. The total surface area of a 6 inch solid cube is 144 square inches.   6.____

7. 1728 cubic feet equal 192 cubic yards.   7.____

8. When the mix proportion for a concrete sidewalk is given as 1:3:5, the numbers give the ratio by volume of cement to sand to coarse aggregate.   8.____

9. When oily waste rags are not in use, it is good practice to store them in self-closing metal containers.   9.____

10. The CHIEF purpose of a trap under a plumbing fixture is to act as a seal against sewer gas.   10.____

11. If a rectangular frame measures 12 inches long and 9 inches wide, the length of its diagonal is 21 inches.   11.____

12. Threads on the inside of metal pipes are usually cut with dies.   12.____

13. A screwdriver is the proper tool to drive a lag screw into place.   13.____

14. The diameter of one inch pipe is measured from the outside of the pipe.   14.____

15. If the counterweights of the top sash of a window are too heavy, more exertion will be necessary to close that half of the window.   15.____

16. Glazed tile should be wet prior to being laid.   16.____

17. The striking plate is part of a lockset.   17.____

18. A casement window usually slides up and down.   18.____

19. An escutcheon plate is part of a lockset.   19.____

20. When using a hand saw, it is good practice to pull up rather than push down the saw when starting the first stroke.   20.____

21. Hickory is a very brittle wood. 21._____

22. Timber which is continually wet will not rot as soon as timber which is alternately wet and dry. 22._____

23. A nosing is the projecting edge of a stair tread. 23._____

24. When sawing wood marked off with a pencil line, the saw should be driven through the center of the pencil line. 24._____

25. One 45 degree elbow fitting will make a right angle. 25._____

26. The MOST probable cause of the water of a flush tank of a toilet continuing to flow after the flushing has stopped is that the rubber ball fails to seat properly. 26._____

27. Nails driven with the grain of the wood do not hold as well as when driven across the grain. 27._____

28. Usually sandpapering of wood should be done with the grain. 28._____

29. After concrete sidewalks are poured in the open air, they are usually covered with straw or paper in order to give a bright color to the sidewalk. 29._____

30. To prevent screws from splitting the wood when they are being driven, it is good practice to drill a small hole first. 30._____

31. The PRINCIPAL purpose of a leader is to carry away sewage from a building. 31._____

32. The PRINCIPAL purpose of a hacksaw is to cut thin wood. 32._____

33. The board around a room at the bottom of the walls is known as a baseboard. 33._____

34. Clay tiles, when used on the interior of buildings, are usually set in Portland cement mortar. 34._____

35. Before window glass is set in wooden window sashes, putty should be placed in the rebates of the sash. 35._____

36. Clear window glass is made in ONLY one thickness. 36._____

37. Glass which is to be set in wooden sash windows should be cut to the exact measurements between the sashes. 37._____

38. Three eighths (3/8") of an inch is equivalent to .0375". 38._____

39. Nipples are short pieces of pipe threaded only on one end. 39._____

40. Pipe fittings which connect pipes so that they may be at an angle to each other are known as elbows. 40._____

41. Solder is a mixture of lead and brass. 41._____

42. A yellow flame in the burner of a gas range usually indicates that the proper amount of air for combustion is present. 42._____

43. Gaskets are generally used to relieve clogged drain pipes. 43.____

44. The PRINCIPAL purpose of galvanizing iron is to prevent rust. 44.____

45. When driving a long nail into a piece of wood, it is good practice to start hammering with light blows. 45.____

46. If a maintenance man is to remove a door having two hinges from its frame, he should FIRST remove the lower hinge. 46.____

47. If a 10 ampere fuse blows out constantly, it should be replaced with a 15 ampere fuse. 47.____

48. When grinding a tool, the stone should revolve towards the bevel edge of the tool that is pressed against it. 48.____

49. The upright members of a wooden door are known as rails. 49.____

50. Casement windows are balanced with weights. 50.____

KEY (CORRECT ANSWERS)

1. T	11. F	21. F	31. F	41. F
2. F	12. F	22. T	32. F	42. F
3. T	13. F	23. T	33. T	43. F
4. F	14. F	24. F	34. T	44. T
5. T	15. F	25. F	35. T	45. T
6. F	16. T	26. T	36. F	46. T
7. F	17. T	27. T	37. F	47. F
8. T	18. F	28. T	38. F	48. T
9. T	19. T	29. F	39. F	49. F
10. T	20. T	30. T	40. T	50. F

TEST 2

DIRECTIONS: Each question consists of a statement. You are to indicate whether the statement is TRUE (T) or FALSE (F). *PRINT THE LETTER OF THE CORRECT ANSWER IN THE SPACE AT THE RIGHT.*

1. Stillson wrench is another name for a monkey wrench. 1.____

2. To draw a nail from a board with a claw hammer, the greatest drawing power will result when the handle of the hammer is held at the end farthest from the head. 2.____

3. To remove paint spots from a wooden desk, it is BETTER to use turpentine rather than linseed oil. 3.____

4. The water level in the flushing tank of a water closet should not be lower than the overflow opening, 4.____

5. The BEST method of repairing cracks in a toilet bowl of solid porcelain is to putty them. 5.____

6. When making concrete by hand, the sand and cement should be nixed together before adding water. 6.____

7. To lift a heavy object from the floor, a person should keep the legs straight and do the lifting with his back. 7.____

8. It is not good practice to report accidents on a job when they do not seem to be serious. 8.____

9. Tools used by workmen should generally be cleaned before storing away each night. 9.____

10. If a maintenance man receives an order from his foreman to do a job which he does not understand, he should use his own judgment and go ahead with the job. 10.____

11. The legs of a compass should be spread 5 inches apart in order to draw a circle with a diameter 5 inches. 11.____

12. A box measuring 18 inches square and 16 inches deep will have a volume of 36 cubic feet. 12.____

13. When setting glass in windows, it is good practice to give the wood a coat of linseed oil before applying the putty. 13.____

14. A nail set is used to drive wood screws beneath the surface of the floor. 14.____

15. When replacing a door in its frame, the top hinge should be attached before the bottom hinge. 15.____

16. A ripsaw is the proper tool for cutting metal pipe. 16.____

17. In cold weather the temperature of a room may be lowered due to conduction of heat through window glass. 17.____

18. The object of marking off sidewalks into rectangular slabs is to prevent pedestrians slipping on the completed walk. 18.____

19. The CHIEF purpose in keeping tools and supplies in orderly manner is to discourage theft of the tools. 19.____

20. The horizontal members of a wooden door are known as rails. 20.____

21. A wood chisel is sharpened only on one side. 21.____

22. A screwdriver is the proper tool for driving a nail below the surface of the wood. 22.____

23. Putty for window glazing is usually made of cement and linseed oil. 23.____

24. Hickory is a suitable wood for handles of hammers. 24.____

25. The number on the saw blade of a carpenter's saw near the handle indicates the width of the saw at the point. 25.____

26. The vertical part of stair steps is called the riser. 26.____

27. A reamer is the CORRECT tool with which to put threads on a pipe. 27.____

28. A person should face the ladder as he descends on it. 28.____

29. A center punch is used for marking points on metal at which holes are to be drilled. 29.____

30. A stud bolt has a square head. 30.____

31. The teeth of saws are usually bent sideways alternately to prevent saw binding in the cut slot. 31.____

32. When inserting a pane of window glass in a wooden window sash, glazier's points should be forced into the sash after the puttying has been completed. 32.____

33. Lead poisoning may result after eating meals while red lead or lead filings are under the nails of the hands of the worker. 33.____

34. A coupling is a pipe fitting with internal threads. 34.____

35. A tee joint for pipe has 3 openings. 35.____

36. A die is generally used to cut threads in a nut. 36.____

37. Glass is a good electrical conductor. 37.____

38. Small nails used in fine work are called rivets. 38.____

39. A fuse wire should melt less readily than the wiring in the circuit which it protects. 39.____

40. The diameter of a circle is equal to half its circumference. 40.____

41. The unit of electrical resistance is the ampere. 41.____

42. Where only a short swing of the handle is possible, the ratchet type wrench is best used. 42.____

43. Iron coated with tin is called galvanized iron. 43.____

44. An advantage of cast iron is that it bends very easily but does not break. 44.____

45. Monel metal rusts very quickly. 45.____

46. A *compass* saw is best used for cutting heavy boards. 46.____

47. Brads are used to fasten heavy boards together. 47.____

48. When used in connection with nails, *penny* refers to quality. 48.____

49. An expansion bolt is usually used to allow for expansion and contraction due to climatic conditions. 49.____

50. The French polish finish is the FINEST shellac finish that there is. 50.____

KEY (CORRECT ANSWERS)

1. F	11. F	21. T	31. T	41. F
2. T	12. F	22. F	32. F	42. T
3. T	13. T	23. F	33. T	43. F
4. F	14. F	24. T	34. T	44. F
5. F	15. T	25. F	35. T	45. F
6. T	16. F	26. T	36. F	46. F
7. F	17. T	27. F	37. T	47. F
8. F	18. F	28. T	38. F	48. F
9. T	19. F	29. T	39. F	49. F
10. F	20. T	30. F	40. F	50. T

TEST 3

DIRECTIONS: Each question consists of a statement. You are to indicate whether the statement is TRUE (T) or FALSE (F). *PRINT THE LETTER OF THE CORRECT ANSWER IN THE SPACE AT THE RIGHT.*

1. To lay out very precise work on wood, it is BEST to use a chalk line. 1._____
2. A ripsaw is BEST used for cutting wood across the grain. 2._____
3. Beach sand, because of its uniform grain, will make a dense and strong concrete. 3._____
4. A *union* is the same as a *coupling* in plumbing. 4._____
5. A valve that permits free passage of water through a pipe or valve in one direction, but prevents a reversal of flow, is called a check valve. 5._____
6. Iron or steel fittings used with brass or copper pipe would cause an electrical action that would be unsatisfactory. 6._____
7. Brass and copper are USUALLY softer than iron or steel. 7._____
8. While pipe is being cut to length and threaded, it is held securely in place usually by a pipe vise. 8._____
9. With respect to water closets, pressure flush valves are usually used without a tank. 9._____
10. Troubles resulting from low velocity of liquids flowing through horizontal pipes are greatly lessened by giving these pipes a downward pitch toward the soil. 10._____
11. Water is delivered to the building under pressure from a street main. The pipe coming into the building is usually called the downtake pipe. 11._____
12. Elbows usually have female threads at both ends. 12._____
13. Extensive tests have shown that the strength of timber is increased as its moisture content is decreased. 13._____
14. Thawing a frozen water pipe by means of a blowtorch is highly recommended. 14._____
15. Heat applied to a frozen water pipe should be applied first at the middle of the frozen part. 15._____
16. Water closet traps may be cleaned with a tool called a closet auger. This is usually operated by compressed air. 16._____
17. With respect to faucet washers, leather and fibre washers are satisfactory for cold water, but composition materials generally last longer on the hot water side. 17._____
18. A pipe cutter leaves a larger burr on the outside of a pipe than on the inside. 18._____
19. In threading pipe, dirt and chips in the stock and die will result in imperfect threads. 19._____
20. The burr resulting from cutting pipe is BEST removed by a pipe tapper. 20._____

21. With respect to pipe, the abbreviation I.P.S. means iron pipe shape. 21.____

22. Caustic potash when used as a drain pipe solvent will NOT damage aluminum. 22.____

23. Any pipe which carries the discharge from one or more water closets to the house drain is called a soil pipe. 23.____

24. A vent stack is a vertical pipe whose primary purpose is to allow circulation of air to and from any other piping in the drainage system of the building. 24.____

25. Evaporation may gradually reduce the depth of trap water in case a fixture remains unused for long periods. 25.____

26. The rubber ball stopper in a flush tank is held in place normally by air pressure. 26.____

27. In water closets an overflow tube allows water to flow into the closet bowl should the ball cock fail to close and the level rises too high in the tank. 27.____

28. When the ground seat in a compression faucet has become pitted or grooved, the seat should be dressed down true with a reamer. 28.____

29. A chamfer is a kind of bevel. 29.____

30. A corrugated fastener for joining two pieces of wood can sometimes be used in place of a nail.
It should be driven by heavy blows from a heavy hammer. 30.____

31. No. 1 sandpaper is finer than number 4 sandpaper. 31.____

32. To *rod* a sewer pipe means to support the sewer pipe with reinforcing metal rods. 32.____

33. *T* and *G,* when applied to lumber, means tested and guaranteed. 33.____

34. When a screwdriver is used on a small object, the object should be held in the palm of the hand. 34.____

35. An oval faced hammer is BEST for driving nails. 35.____

36. Metal sash chains are usually of the flat link type. 36.____

37. A casement window can swing only one way, and that way is out. 37.____

38. The mark *UL* on electrical equipment usually means universal license. 38.____

39. Every door closing or checking device must be mounted overhead on the door. 39.____

40. A wash basin with a pop up drain always has a stopper and chain. 40.____

41. A fusible plug is usually used to make a temporary repair on a leaking water pipe. 41.____

42. To be effective, a thermostat must always have a clock connected with it. 42.____

43. Wood with narrow annual rings is denser and stronger than wood with wide annual rings. 43.____

44. BX in the electrical industry means best grade. 44.____

45. A sub-metering device means a device usually buried and underground in the street.   45.____
46. An oscillating fan is designed to run faster automatically as the room temperature rises.   46.____
47. An electrical cooking stove requires a *booster* to light a burner.   47.____
48. A universal motor is designed to operate with either A.C. or D.C. power.   48.____
49. An A.C. fuse will NOT operate on D.C.   49.____
50. Special circuit wiring is required for the installation of fluorescent lighting fixtures.   50.____

KEY (CORRECT ANSWERS)

1. F	11. F	21. F	31. T	41. F
2. F	12. T	22. F	32. F	42. F
3. F	13. T	23. T	33. F	43. T
4. F	14. F	24. T	34. F	44. F
5. T	15. F	25. T	35. F	45. F
6. T	16. F	26. F	36. T	46. F
7. T	17. T	27. T	37. F	47. F
8. T	18. F	28. F	38. F	48. T
9. T	19. T	29. T	39. F	49. F
10. T	20. F	30. F	40. F	50. F

TEST 4

DIRECTIONS: Each question consists of a statement. You are to indicate whether the statement is TRUE (T) or FALSE (F). *PRINT THE LETTER OF THE CORRECT ANSWER IN THE SPACE AT THE RIGHT.*

1. *Scotch* tape is preferable to friction tape for the splicing of electrical conductors. 1.____
2. With respect to passenger elevators, car doors and shaft doors are the same. 2.____
3. A pendant fixture is a fixture hanging or suspended. 3.____
4. A rectifier changes A.C. to D.C. current. 4.____
5. A knife switch is used to cut small sections of wire from a spool of wire. 5.____
6. Domestic electric bills are usually rendered for kilowatt hours consumed. 6.____
7. When lamps are connected in series, if one goes out, all go out. 7.____
8. A household iron usually consumes about 110 watts. 8.____
9. The dry cell battery supplies alternating current. 9.____
10. On the dry cell battery, one terminal is called the positive and the other is called the negative. 10.____
11. An annunciator is a device to change the voltage of a current of electricity. 11.____
12. The average household electric bulb contains air under heavy pressure. 12.____
13. Insulators offer high resistance to the flow of electricity. 13.____
14. The smaller the wire, the larger the current carrying capacity of the wire. 14.____
15. #14 wire is smaller than #8 wire. 15.____
16. Transformers can operate only on A.C. 16.____
17. Some cartridge fuses are renewable by replacing the fuse element. 17.____
18. A *short* in a circuit should *blow* the fuse. 18.____
19. A circuit breaker is a type of conduit. 19.____
20. A miter box is used to store small nails, washers, and tools on the job. 20.____
21. When a hidden edge is shown on a drawing, it is represented by a dotted line. 21.____
22. A rasp is a kind of heavy hammer. 22.____
23. *Green* lumber is lumber not well seasoned. 23.____
24. A dowel is usually triangular in shape. 24.____
25. Monkey wrenches usually have jaws with teeth. 25.____

26. The only material that can cut glass is a diamond, or diamond chip.   26.____
27. An extension ladder and a step ladder are the same.   27.____
28. A turnbuckle is a type of general purpose wrench.   28.____
29. Terrazzo is a kind of concealed joint used in expensive cabinet work.   29.____
30. A burr is a kind of metal measuring tape.   30.____
31. Armored cable is cable with a soft outer covering but with very heavy inside wire.   31.____
32. Continued use of a portable electric room heater will *use up* the oxygen in a small closed room quicker than a gas heater.   32.____
33. Plate glass is generally superior to sheet glass for windows.   33.____
34. White pine is a harder wood than white oak.   34.____
35. Chestnut is usually considered an *open grained* wood.   35.____
36. #30 sheet iron is thicker than #14.   36.____
37. Semi-vitreous tiles are generally harder than vitreous tiles.   37.____
38. One disadvantage of interlocking rubber tiling is that it is *noisy* in use.   38.____
39. A *light* of glass is the same as a *pane* of glass.   39.____
40. The scratch coat of plaster is the last coat to be applied.   40.____
41. The riser pipe in a heating system is usually horizontal.   41.____
42. With reference to wire specifications, AWG means American Wire Gage.   42.____
43. Electric motors are never rated in terms of horsepower.   43.____
44. The use of self-closing water faucets should help reduce water waste.   44.____
45. *Push button* elevators are manufactured only by the Otis Elevator Company.   45.____
46. Gas bills are usually computed on the basis of cubic feet consumed.   46.____
47. With respect to pipe, I.D. usually means inside diameter.   47.____
48. Graphite is sometimes used as a lubricant.   48.____
49. A blow torch can burn gasoline only.   49.____
50. Bronze is composed CHIEFLY of copper and tin.   50.____

KEY (CORRECT ANSWERS)

1. F	11. F	21. T	31. F	41. F
2. F	12. F	22. F	32. F	42. T
3. T	13. T	23. T	33. T	43. F
4. T	14. F	24. F	34. F	44. T
5. F	15. T	25. F	35. T	45. F
6. T	16. T	26. F	36. F	46. T
7. T	17. T	27. F	37. F	47. T
8. F	18. T	28. F	38. F	48. T
9. F	19. F	29. F	39. T	49. F
10. T	20. F	30. F	40. F	50. T

EXAMINATION SECTION
TEST 1

DIRECTIONS: Each question or incomplete statement is followed by several suggested answers or completions. Select the one that BEST answers the question or completes the statement. *PRINT THE LETTER OF THE CORRECT ANSWER IN THE SPACE AT THE RIGHT.*

1. The composition of plumber's solder for wiping is APPROXIMATELY (ratio of tin to lead) 1.____

   A. 40-60   B. 50-50   C. 60-40   D. 70-30

2. A device used to lift sewage to the level of a sewer from a floor below the sewer grade is known as a(n) 2.____

   A. elevator   B. ejector   C. sump   D. conveyer

3. A check valve in a piping system will 3.____

   A. permit excessive pressures in a boiler
   B. eliminate water hammer
   C. permit water to flow in only one direction
   D. control the rate of flow of water

4. The chemical MOST frequently used to clean drains clogged with grease is 4.____

   A. muriatic acid   B. soda ash
   C. ammonia   D. caustic soda

5. To test for leaks in a newly installed C.I. waste stack, 5.____

   A. oil of peppermint is poured into the top of the stack
   B. smoke under pressure is pumped into the stack
   C. a water meter is used to measure the water flow
   D. dye is placed in the system at the top of the stack

6. When installing a catch basin, the outlet should be located 6.____

   A. at the same level as the inlet
   B. above the inlet
   C. below the inlet
   D. at the invert

7. The copper float in a low down water tank is perforated so that water enters the ball. As a result, the tank will 7.____

   A. flush once, and then will not operate again
   B. not flush at all
   C. not flush completely
   D. continue to flush, but water will be wasted

8. If water leaks from the stem of a faucet when the faucet is opened, the _____ should be 8.____

   A. faucet; replaced   B. cap nut; rethreaded
   C. seat; reground   D. packing; replaced

49

9. In a hot water heating system, it may be necessary to *bleed* radiators to

   A. relieve high steam pressure
   B. permit entrapped, air to escape
   C. allow condensate to return to the boiler
   D. drain off waste water

10. When painting raw wood, puttying of nail holes should be done

    A. 24 hours before the prime coat
    B. immediately before the prime coat
    C. after the prime coat and before the second coat
    D. after the second coat and before the finish

11. In general, the one of the following that will dry *tack free* in the SHORTEST time is

    A. lacquer   B. varnish   C. enamel   D. oil paint

12. The *vehicle* MOST frequently used in paints for exterior wood surfaces is

    A. white lead   B. linseed oil
    C. japan   D. varnish

13. Painting of an interior plastered wall is usually delayed until the plaster is dry. If this practice is NOT followed, the paint might

    A. chalk   B. fade   C. run   D. blister

14. A *sealer* applied over knots and pitch streaks to prevent *bleeding* through paint is

    A. shellac   B. lacquer
    C. coal tar   D. carnauba wax

15. Painting of outside steel in near freezing (32° F) weather is poor practice MAINLY because

    A. the paint will not dry properly
    B. ice will form in the thinner
    C. more paint is required
    D. paint fumes are dangerous

16. When repainting exterior woodwork that has a glossy finish, good adhesion of paint is BEST obtained by first

    A. *washing* the work with diluted lye
    B. *dulling* the work with sandpaper
    C. *warming* the work with an electric heater
    D. *roughening* the work with a rasp

17. The one of the following methods of cleaning steelwork prior to painting that is NOT commonly used on exterior work, such as bridges, is

    A. sandblasting   B. flame cleaning
    C. wire brushing   D. pickling

18. When spraying oil paints, the type of gun and nozzle preferred is a _____ feed gun, _____ mix nozzle.

   A. pressure; internal
   B. pressure, external
   C. syphon; internal
   D. syphon; external

19. When opening a bag of cement, you find that the cement is lumpy. The cement should be

   A. discarded and not used at all
   B. crushed before placing in the mixer
   C. used as is since the mixer will grind it
   D. well mixed with water and stored overnight before using

20. A 1:2:4 concrete mix by volume is specified. If 6 cubic feet of cement is to be used in the mix, the volume of sand to use is, in cubic feet,

   A. 3   B. 6   C. 12   D. 24

21. Honeycombing in concrete is BEST prevented by

   A. increasing water-cement ratio
   B. heating concrete in cold weather
   C. using mechanical vibrators
   D. adding calcium chloride

22. When a lightweight concrete is required, the one of the following that is COMMONLY used as an aggregate is

   A. gravel   B. brick chips   C. stone   D. cinders

23. A rubbed finish on concrete is USUALLY obtained by use of a

   A. carborundum brick
   B. garnet sanding belt
   C. fibre brush and wax
   D. pad of steel wool

24. A copper strip is frequently embedded in the concrete across a construction joint in a concrete wall. The purpose of this is to

   A. make a watertight joint
   B. bond the two parts of the wall together
   C. prevent unequal settlement
   D. retard temperature cracking

25. In brickwork laid in common bond, a header course USUALLY occurs in every _____ course.

   A. 2nd   B. 4th   C. 6th   D. 8th

26. Pointing of brickwork refers to

   A. cutting brick to fit
   B. patching mortar joints
   C. attaching brick veneer
   D. arranging brick in an arch

27. Furring is applied to brick walls to

    A. strengthen the wall
    B. waterproof the wall
    C. provide ventilation to prevent condensation
    D. provide a base for lathing

28. The FIRST coat in plaster work is *scratched* in order to

    A. remove excess plaster
    B. smooth the base for the second coat
    C. provide a bond for the second coat
    D. strengthen the base coat

29. An alloy used where resistance to corrosion is important is

    A. tungsten   B. mild steel   C. monel   D. tin

30. The size of iron pipe is given in terms of its nominal

    A. weight   B. inside diameter
    C. outside diameter   D. wall thickness

31. When preparing surfaces to be soldered, the FIRST step is

    A. tinning   B. sweating   C. heating   D. cleaning

32. To test for leaks in an acetylene torch, it is BEST that one use

    A. soapy water   B. a match
    C. a gas with a strong odor D. a pressure gauge

33. One advantage of using a Pittsburgh lock seam when joining two pieces of sheet metal is that, once formed in the shop, it may be assembled anywhere with a

    A. hickey   B. swage   C. template   D. mallet

34. White cast iron is

    A. hard and brittle   B. hard and ductile
    C. ductile and malleable D. brittle and malleable

35. The gage used for measuring copper wire is

    A. U.S. Standard   B. Stubbs
    C. Washburn and Moen   D. Brown and Sharpe

36. The BEST flux to use when soldering copper wires in an electric circuit is

    A. sal ammoniac   B. zinc chloride
    C. rosin   D. borax

37. The spark test, to determine the approximate composition of an unknown metal, is made by

    A. holding the metal against a grinding wheel
    B. striking flint on the unknown metal
    C. connecting wires from a source of electric power to the metal and striking an arc with a bare wire
    D. heating with an oxyacetylene torch

38. The one of the following metals that is MOST commonly used for bearings is   38.____

    A. duraluminum   B. brass   C. babbit   D. lead

39. A *tailstock* is found on a   39.____

    A. drill press   B. shaper   C. planer   D. lathe

40. The BEST lubricant to use when cutting screw threads in steel is   40.____

    A. naphtha   B. 3-in-1 oil
    C. lard oil   D. linseed oil

41. When a high speed cutting tool is required, the tip is frequently made of   41.____

    A. carborundum   B. tungsten carbide
    C. bronze   D. vanadium

42. A nut is turned on a 3/4"-10 bolt.   42.____
    When the nut is turned five complete turns on this bolt, the distance it moves along the bolt

    A. depends on the type of thread   B. is 0.2 inches
    C. is 0.375 inches   D. is 0.5 inches

43. Of the following, the STRONGEST screw thread form is the   43.____

    A. Whitworth   B. Acme
    C. National Standard   D. V

44. *Knurling* refers to   44.____

    A. rolling depressions in a fixed pattern on a cylindrical surface
    B. turning between centers on a lathe
    C. making deep cuts in a flat plate with a milling machine
    D. drilling matching holes in bolt and nut for a cotter pin

45. A special device used to guide the drill as well as to hold the work when drilling is known as a   45.____

    A. dolly   B. jig   C. chuck   D. collet

46. Tools that have a *Morse taper* would be used on a   46.____

    A. milling machine   B. shaper
    C. planer   D. drill press

47. When tapping a blind hole in a plate, the FIRST tap to use is a   47.____

    A. plug   B. bottoming   C. lead   D. taper

48. An important safety practice to remember when cutting a rivet with a chisel is to wear   48.____

    A. leather gloves   B. steel toe shoes
    C. cup goggles   D. a hard hat

49. Electricians working around *live wires* should wear gloves made of   49._____

    A. asbestos   B. metal mesh   C. leather   D. rubber

50. Storage of oily rags presents a safety hazard because of possible   50._____

    A. fire   B. poisonous flames
    C. attraction of rats   D. leakage of oil

KEY (CORRECT ANSWERS)

1.	A	11.	A	21.	C	31.	D	41.	B
2.	B	12.	B	22.	D	32.	A	42.	D
3.	C	13.	D	23.	A	33.	D	43.	B
4.	D	14.	A	24.	A	34.	A	44.	A
5.	B	15.	A	25.	C	35.	B	45.	B
6.	C	16.	B	26.	B	36.	C	46.	D
7.	D	17.	D	27.	D	37.	A	47.	D
8.	D	18.	A	28.	C	38.	C	48.	C
9.	B	19.	A	29.	C	39.	D	49.	D
10.	C	20.	C	30.	B	40.	C	50.	A

TEST 2

DIRECTIONS: Each question or incomplete statement is followed by several suggested answers or completions. Select the one that BEST answers the question or completes the statement. *PRINT THE LETTER OF THE CORRECT ANSWER IN THE SPACE AT THE RIGHT.*

1. *Shimmying* of the front wheels of a truck is MOST frequently caused by 1.____

    A. worn front brake drums
    B. a worn differential gear
    C. a loose steering gear
    D. a dead shock absorber

2. The MOST important reason for maintaining correct air pressure in all tires of a truck is to 2.____

    A. prevent the truck from swerving when brakes are applied
    B. permit the truck to stop quicker in an emergency
    C. provide a smoother ride
    D. prevent excessive wear on the tires

3. The oil gage on the dashboard of a truck indicates 3.____

    A. the amount of oil in the pan
    B. the pressure at which the oil is being pumped
    C. if the oil filter is working
    D. the temperature of the oil in the motor

4. An unbalanced wheel on a truck is corrected by 4.____

    A. bending the rim slightly
    B. adjusting the king pin
    C. changing the ratio of caster to camber
    D. adding small weights to the rim

5. A cold motor on a truck should be warmed up in wintertime by 5.____

    A. turning on the heater and pouring warm water into the radiator
    B. allowing the motor to idle for a few minutes
    C. racing the motor
    D. alternately pressing the gas pedal to the floor and releasing it

6. The brake pedal on a truck goes to the floorboard when pushed. 6.____
   The one of the following that would cause this condition is

    A. air in the hydraulic system
    B. wet brakes
    C. excessive fluid in the cylinders
    D. a loose backing plate

7. The ammeter of a truck indicates no charge during operation even though the battery is 7.____
   run down. To find the fault, the generator field terminal is grounded. The ammeter now shows a charge. The part that is defective is the

    A. generator field coil
    B. armature
    C. brushes
    D. voltage regulator

8. The part used to control the ratio of air and gasoline in a truck engine is the

   A. bogie   B. filter   C. carburetor   D. pump

9. The MAIN purpose of a vacuum booster on a truck engine is to

   A. increase the manifold vacuum
   B. assist windshield wiper operation
   C. provide a steadier fuel flow
   D. govern engine speed

10. The purpose of grounding the frame of an electric motor is to

    A. prevent excessive vibration
    B. eliminate shock hazards
    C. reduce power requirements
    D. prevent overheating

11. The one of the following that is NOT part of an electric motor is a

    A. brush   B. rheostat   C. pole   D. commutator

12. An electrical transformer would be used to

    A. change current from AC to DC
    B. raise or lower the power
    C. raise or lower the voltage
    D. change the frequency

13. The piece of equipment that would be rated in ampere hours is a

    A. storage battery
    B. bus bar
    C. rectifier
    D. capacitor

14. A ballast is a necessity in a(n)

    A. motor generator set
    B. fluorescent lighting system
    C. oil circuit breaker
    D. synchronous converter

15. The power factor in an AC circuit is on when

    A. no current is flowing
    B. the voltage at the source is a minimum
    C. the voltage and current are in phase
    D. there is no load

16.

Neglecting the internal resistance in the battery, the current flowing through the battery shown in the sketch above is _____ amp.

   A. 3   B. 6   C. 9   D. 12

17. When excess current flows, a circuit breaker is opened directly by the action of a   17.____

   A. condenser   B. transistor   C. relay   D. solenoid

18. The MAIN purpose of bridging in building floor construction is to   18.____

   A. spread floor loads evenly to joists
   B. reduce the number of joists required
   C. permit use of thinner subflooring
   D. reduce noise passage through floors

19. Of the following, the material MOST commonly used for subflooring is   19.____

   A. rock lath   B. insulation board
   C. plywood   D. transite

20. In connection with stair construction, the one of the following that is LEAST related to the others is   20.____

   A. tread   B. cap   C. nosing   D. riser

21. The type of nail MOST commonly used in flooring is   21.____

   A. common   B. cut   C. brad   D. casing

22. The edge joint of flooring boards is COMMONLY   22.____

   A. mortise and tenon   B. shiplap
   C. half lap   D. tongue and groove

23. The purpose of a ridge board in building construction is to   23.____

   A. locate corners of a building
   B. keep plaster work smooth
   C. support the ends of roof rafters
   D. conceal openings at the eaves

24. To prevent splintering of wood when using an auger bit,   24.____

   A. the bit should be hollow ground
   B. hold the piece of wood in a vise
   C. clamp a piece of scrap wood to the back of the piece being drilled
   D. use a slow speed on the drill press

25. End grain of a post can be MOST easily planed by use of a _____ plane.   25.____

   A. rafter   B. jack   C. fore   D. block

26. A butt gauge is used when   26.____

   A. hanging doors   B. laying out stairs
   C. making rafter cuts D. framing studs

27. The one of the following grades of sandpaper with the FINEST grit is   27.____

   A. 0   B. 2/0   C. 1/2   D. 1

28. The sum of the following numbers, 3 7/8, 14 1/4, 6 7/16, 22 3/16, 8 1/2 is

    A. 55 1/16   B. 55 1/8   C. 55 3/16   D. 55 1/4

29. The area of the rectangular field shown in the diagram at the right is, in square feet,
    A. 29,456
    B. 29,626
    C. 29,716
    D. 29,836

    437 FT.

    68 ft

30. The cost of material is approximately 3/8ths of the total cost of a certain job. If the total cost of the job is $127.56, then the cost of material is MOST NEARLY

    A. $47.83   B. $48.24   C. $48.65   D. $49.06

31. A blueprint is drawn to a scale of 1/4" = 1'0". A line on the blueprint that is not dimensioned is measured with a ruler and found to be 3 3/8" long.
    The length represented by this line is

    A. 13'2"   B. 13'4"   C. 13'6"   D. 13'8"

32. A maintainer, in repairing a brick wall, spends one-half hour getting materials, forty-three minutes chipping and cleaning the wall, fifteen minutes mixing the mortar, and one hour and twenty-seven minutes in applying the brick and finishing.
    The total time spent on this repair job is _____ hours _____ minute(s).

    A. 2; 45   B. 2; 50   C. 2; 55   D. 3; 0

33. *Employees are responsible for the good care, proper maintenance, and* serviceable condition *of property issued or assigned to their use.*
    As used above, *serviceable condition* means MOST NEARLY

    A. capable of being repaired B. fit for use
    C. ease of handling   D. minimum cost

34. An employee shall be on the alert constantly for potential accident hazards.
    As used above, *potential* means MOST NEARLY

    A. dangerous   B. careless   C. possible   D. frequent

Questions 35-37.

DIRECTIONS: Questions 35 to 37, inclusive, are to be answered in accordance with the following paragraph.

All cement work contracts, more or less, in setting. The contraction in concrete walls and other structures causes fine cracks to develop at regular intervals. The tendency to contract increases in direct proportion to the quantity of cement in the concrete. A rich mixture will contract more than a lean mixture. A concrete wall, which has been made of a very lean mixture and which has been built by filling only about one foot in depth of concrete in the form each day will frequently require close inspection to reveal the cracks.

35. According to the above paragraph,

    A. shrinkage seldom occurs in concrete
    B. shrinkage occurs only in certain types of concrete
    C. by placing concrete at regular intervals, shrinkage may be avoided
    D. it is impossible to prevent shrinkage

36. According to the above paragraph, the one of the factors which reduces shrinkage in concrete is the

    A. volume of concrete in wall
    B. height of each day's pour
    C. length of wall
    D. length and height of wall

37. According to the above paragraph, a rich mixture

    A. pours the easiest
    B. shows the largest amount of cracks
    C. is low in cement content
    D. need not be inspected since cracks are few

Questions 38-39.

DIRECTIONS: Questions 38 and 39 are to be answered in accordance with the following paragraph.

Painting is done to preserve surfaces, and unless the surface is properly prepared, good preservation will not be possible. Apply paint only to clean dry surfaces. After a surface has been scaled, which means that all loose paint and rust are removed by chipping, scraping, and wire brushing, be sure all dust and dirt are completely removed.

38. According to the above paragraph, the MAIN purpose of painting a wall is to _____ the wall.

    A. clean   B. waterproof
    C. protect   D. remove dust from

39. According to the above paragraph,

    A. chipping, scraping, and wire brushing are the only methods permitted for cleaning surfaces
    B. painting is effective only when the surface is clean
    C. scaling refers only to the removal of rust
    D. paint may be applied on wet surfaces

40. The order in which the dimensions of stock are listed on a bill of materials is

    A. thickness, length, and width   B. thickness, width, and length
    C. width, length, and thickness   D. length, thickness, and width

41. The glue that will BEST withstand extreme exposure to moisture and water is _____ glue.

    A. polyvinyl
    B. resorcinol
    C. powdered resin
    D. protein

42. Four board feet of lumber, listed at $350.00 per M, will cost

    A. $3.50   B. $1.40   C. $1.30   D. $4.00

43. The cap iron or chip breaker stiffens the plane iron and

    A. protects the cutting edge
    B. curls the shaving
    C. regulates the thickness of the shaving
    D. reduces mouth gap

44. Coping-saw blades have teeth shaped like those on a _____ saw.

    A. dovetail   B. crosscut   C. back   D. rip

45. Of the following, the claw hammer that is BEST suited for general use in a woodworking shop is the _____ claw.

    A. straight
    B. bell-faced curved
    C. plain-faced curved
    D. adze eye curved

46. The natural binder which cements wood fibers together and makes wood solid is

    A. cellulose
    B. lignin
    C. alpha-cellulose
    D. trichocarpa

47. The plane that is BEST suited for trimming the bottom of a dado or lap joint is the _____ plane.

    A. block   B. router   C. rabbet   D. core-box

48. Brads are fasteners that are similar to _____ nails.

    A. escutcheon
    B. box
    C. finishing
    D. duplex head

49. The plane in which the plane iron is inserted with its bevel in the up position is the _____ plane.

    A. fore   B. rabbet   C. block   D. circular

50. Coating materials used to protect wood against fire USUALLY contain a water soluble fire-retardant such as

    A. ammonium chloride
    B. sodium perborate
    C. sodium silicate
    D. sal soda

KEY (CORRECT ANSWERS)

1. C	11. B	21. B	31. C	41. B
2. D	12. C	22. D	32. C	42. B
3. B	13. A	23. C	33. B	43. B
4. D	14. B	24. C	34. C	44. D
5. B	15. C	25. D	35. D	45. B
6. A	16. A	26. A	36. B	46. B
7. D	17. D	27. B	37. B	47. B
8. C	18. A	28. D	38. C	48. C
9. B	19. C	29. C	39. B	49. C
10. B	20. B	30. A	40. B	50. C

EXAMINATION SECTION
TEST 1

DIRECTIONS: Each question or incomplete statement is followed by several suggested answers or completions. Select the one that BEST answers the question or completes the statement. *PRINT THE LETTER OF THE CORRECT ANSWER IN THE SPACE AT THE RIGHT.*

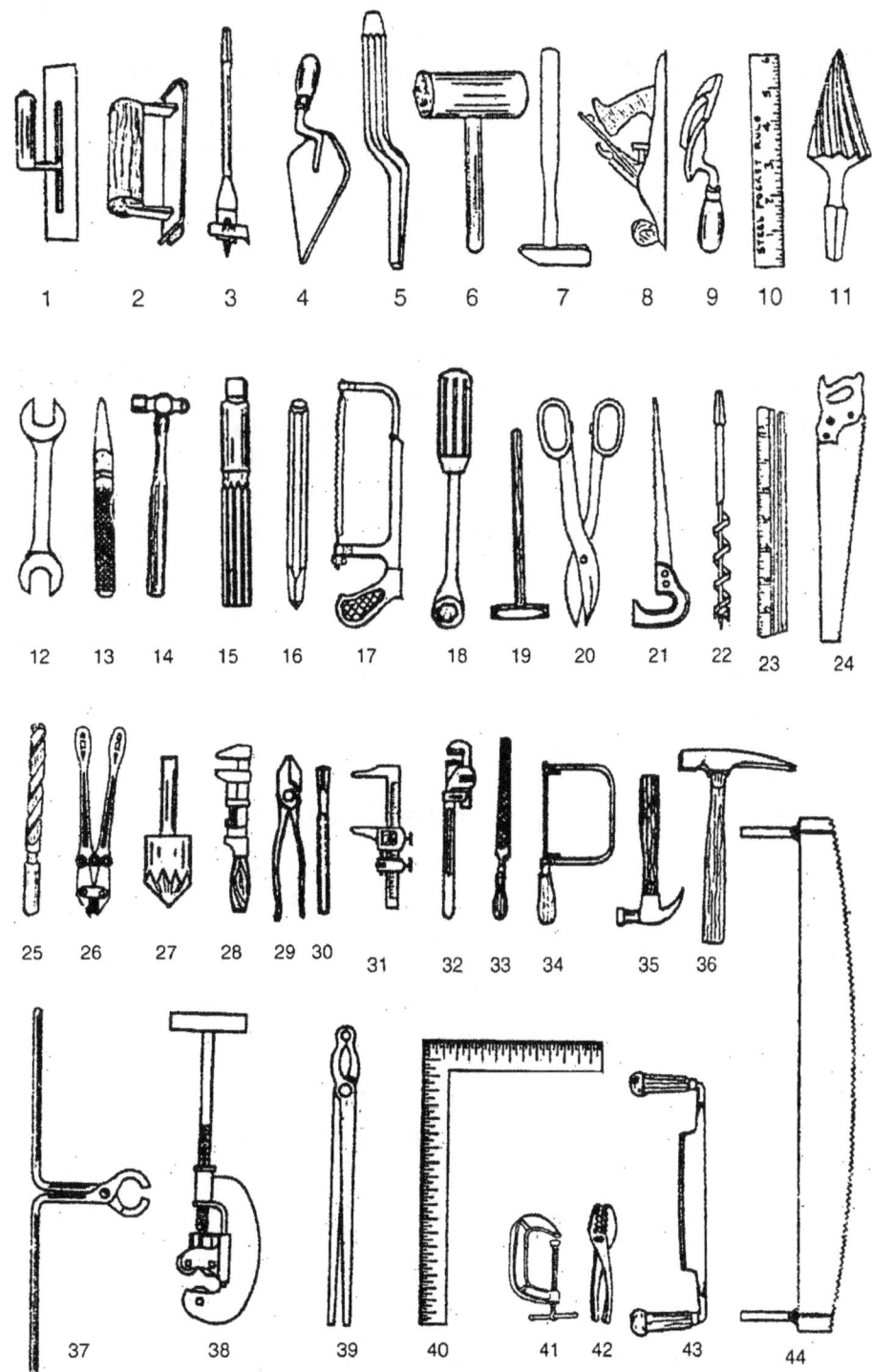

63

1. Of the following, which group of three tools is used *most nearly* in the same way?

   A. Tools 4, 21, 39
   B. Tools 11, 16, 42
   C. Tools 14, 35, 36
   D. Tools 5, 6, 13

2. If you want to cut a disc out of sheet metal, you should use tool no.

   A. 20   B. 26   C. 29   D. 38

3. Tool number 25 is ordinarily NOT used alone; it should be used with tool no.

   A. 28
   B. 35
   C. 39
   D. another tool not pictured

4. To split a brick in half you should FIRST chip the line of division all the way around the brick with tool no.

   A. 14   B. 24   C. 34   D. 36

5. To repair wide cracks in a wood floor you should glue a thin strip of wood into the crack and then level it even with the surrounding floor surface. To level this strip of wood you should use tool no.

   A. 1   B. 8   C. 24   D. 33

6. To smooth a newly laid concrete surface so that it is free of ripples and marks, you should use tool no.

   A. 1   B. 6   C. 8   D. 9

7. To measure the *outside* diameter of a section of pipe MOST accurately, the tool that should be used is tool no.

   A. 10   B. 23   C. 31   D. 40

8. The BEST tool to use to cut a curved pattern in a 1/4 inch-thick sheet of plywood is tool no.

   A. 17   B. 24   C. 34   D. 43

9. If you, as a member of a repair crew, plan to cut a rectangular piece of plywood measuring 18" x 12" out of a larger rectangular piece measuring 30" x 24", the tool that will BEST help lay out the lines and check the angles is number

   A. 10   B. 23   C. 31   D. 40

10. Either end of tool 12 can be *properly* used for the purpose of

    A. fitting into the handle of another tool
    B. turning nuts or bolts
    C. laying out angles
    D. pulling nails

11. Tools 22, 24, 35 and 40 have in common that fact that they are used *primarily* in

    A. masonry
    B. plumbing
    C. sheet metal work
    D. woodworking

12. Which tool requires the use of BOTH hands on the tool to operate it properly? 12.____
    A. Tool 8 B. Tool 12 C. Tool 20 D. Tool 24

13. Of the following, the tool designed to be used for turning nuts of various sizes is tool no. 13.____
    A. 19 B. 28 C. 29 D. 31

14. To cut a section of pipe to the required length, the MOST appropriate tool is number 14.____
    A. 20 B. 29 C. 31 D. 38

15. In the picture below of a roof, which one of the numbered arrows points to the "flashing"? 15.____
    A. 1 B. 2 C. 3 D. 4

16. The function of glazier's points is to 16.____
    A. keep the putty from dirtying the glass
    B. make it easy to cut glass in a straight line
    C. hold a pane of glass in place
    D. aid in applying putty evenly around the glass

17. It is *desirable* for a putty knife used for patching plaster cracks to be flexible because a flexible putty knife 17.____
    A. makes it difficult for the user to cut his hands while applying the plaster
    B. is easier to keep clean than one made of rigid material
    C. can press the patching materials into the crack, filling it completely
    D. makes it possible to pick up the exact amount of plaster required

18. Using a fuse with a *larger* rated capacity than that of the circuit is 18.____
    A. *advisable;* such use prevents the fuse from blowing
    B. *advisable;* larger capacity fuses last longer than smaller capacity fuses
    C. *inadvisable;* larger capacity fuses are more expensive than smaller capacity fuses
    D. *inadvisable;* such use may cause a fire

19. You can MOST easily tell when a screw-in type fuse has blown because the center of the strip of metal in the fuse is 19.____
    A. broken B. visible
    C. nicked D. cool to the touch

20. In the picture below, which of the numbered arrows points to the door "jamb"? 20.____

   A. 1　　　　　B. 2　　　　　C. 3　　　　　D. 4

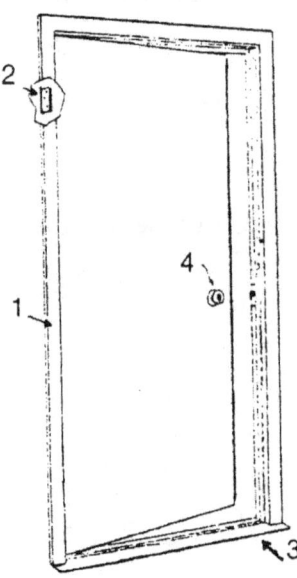

21. Of the following, the MAIN reason why flashing is used in the building trade is to make an area 21.____

   A. decorative　　B. watertight　　C. level　　D. heat-resistant

22. To prepare a ready-mixed concrete material for use, you FIRST add 22.____

   A. gravel　　B. salt　　C. sand　　D. water

23. When working on wet floors with an electrically powered tool, additional safety against electric shock can BEST be provided by 23.____

   A. a longer electric cord　　B. an AC-DC converter
   C. rubber gloves　　　　　　D. loose clothing

24. Which one of the wrenches pictured below is designed to grip round pipes in making plumbing repairs? 24.____

   A. 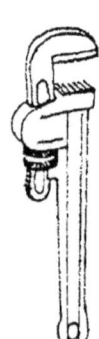　　B. 　　C. 　　D.

25. Which one of the saws pictured below would be BEST to use to cut steel bar stock?   25._____

   A.   B.
   C.   D.

26. Which one of the hammers pictured below is a claw hammer?   26._____

   A.   B.   C.   D.

27. The terms "dovetail" and "dowel" are used to describe types of   27._____

   A. glues   B. joints   C. clamps   D. tile

28. A three-prong plug on a power tool used on a 120-volt line indicates that the tool   28._____

   A. may be grounded against electric shock
   B. is provided with additional power through the third prong
   C. has a defect and should be returned
   D. is adaptable for use with AC or DC current

29. A bit and brace should be used to   29._____

   A. saw wood   B. glue wood
   C. drill holes   D. support or hold work

30. Which of the following would ordinarily occur FIRST in a toilet tank after the handle is pushed down to flush the toilet?   30._____

   A. Float ball drops with water level, opening the ballcock assembly through which fresh water flows into the tank
   B. Tank ball sinks slowly into place
   C. Rising water pushes the float ball up until it closes the ballcock assembly, shutting off the supply of fresh water when the tank is full
   D. The tank ball lifts, opening the outlet so water can flow from tank to bowl

KEY (CORRECT ANSWERS)

1.	C	16.	C
2.	A	17.	C
3.	D	18.	D
4.	D	19.	A
5.	B	20.	A
6.	A	21.	B
7.	C	22.	D
8.	C	23.	C
9.	D	24.	A
10.	B	25.	B
11.	D	26.	C
12.	A	27.	B
13.	B	28.	A
14.	D	29.	C
15.	B	30.	D

TEST 2

DIRECTIONS: Each question or incomplete statement is followed by several suggested answers or completions. Select the one that BEST answers the question or completes the statement. *PRINT THE LETTER OF THE CORRECT ANSWER IN THE SPACE AT THE RIGHT.*

1. Of the following, the MAIN reason for clear glass doors to have a painted design about four and one-half feet above the floor is to   1.____

   A. look attractive
   B. prevent glare
   C. improve safety
   D. make damage, if any, less noticeable

2. When using a wrench to make a repair on a faucet, it is a good idea to cover the wrench with rags in order to   2.____

   A. protect the finish on the faucet
   B. get a closer fit over the faucet
   C. get a better grip on the wrench
   D. get a better grip on the faucet

3. The length of the screw in the sketch below is *most nearly*   3.____

   A. 1 7/8"   B. 2"   C. 2 1/4"   D. 2 5/16"

   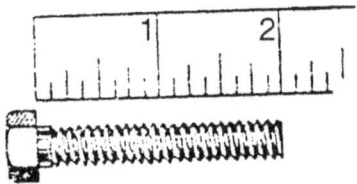

4. Panel doors may have horns which must be cut off before the door is hung. In the sketch below, the arrow which indicates a horn is labeled number   4.____

   A. 1   B. 2   C. 3   D. 4

   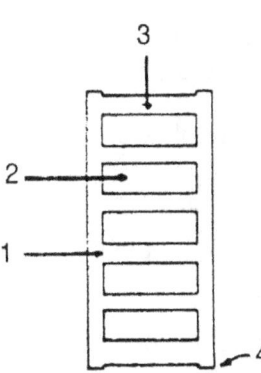

69

5. To "shim a hinge" means to   5._____

   A. swing the hinge from side to side
   B. paint the hinge
   C. polish the hinge
   D. raise up the hinge

6. To hold work that is being planed, sawed, drilled, shaped, sharpened or riveted, you   6._____
   should use a

   A. punch   B. rasp   C. reamer   D. vise

7. A good deal of the trouble caused by faulty and worn locks and hinges can be avoided by   7._____
   proper lubrication.
   The tool you would use to lubricate locks and hinges is

   A.   B.   C.   D.

8. The terms ALLIGATORING, BLISTERING, and PEELING refer to   8._____

   A. carpentry   B. masonry   C. painting   D. plumbing

9. The terms BAT and STRETCHER refer to   9._____

   A. carpentry   B. glazing   C. masonry   D. painting

10. Ladders which are used to extend as high as 60 feet are called   10._____

    A. extension ladders   B. portable ladders
    C. single-section ladders   D. stepladders

11. Of the following, the MOST important advantage that Plexiglass has over regular glass,   11._____
    when used in windows, is that it

    A. is available in a wide range of thicknesses
    B. is easier to clean
    C. offers greater resistance to breakage
    D. offers greater resistance to scratches

12. Clutch-head, offset, Phillips and spiral-ratchet all are different types of   12._____

    A. drills   B. files   C. wrenches   D. screwdrivers

13. Of the following, the MOST important reason for keeping tools in perfect working order is   13._____
    to make sure

    A. the proper tool is being used for the required work
    B. the tools can be operated safely
    C. each employee can repair a variety of building defects
    D. no employee uses a tool for his private use

14. When repairing a hole in a leaking pipe which of the following should be done FIRST?   14._____

   A. Wrap tape around the hole
   B. Turn off the water supply
   C. Tighten a clamp around the hole
   D. Seal the hole with epoxy

15. Freshly cut threads on pipe should be handled with caution *mainly* because the threads   15._____

   A. are the weakest section of the pipe and break easily
   B. do not give a firm handhold for carrying
   C. make a tight seal around a joint
   D. are always sharp

16. When a repair worker must enter a confined space through a small opening, it is a GOOD idea to attach a rope to his body *mainly* because the   16._____

   A. rope reduces unnecessary strain on the body
   B. rope may provide a way to reach the worker in an emergency
   C. worker will be able to get to areas that are not easily reached
   D. worker may be able to use the rope to remove debris from the work space

17. Hitting the handle of a screw driver with a hammer to remove an imbedded screw is a   17._____

   A. *good* practice, since it supplies the necessary force to get the screw started
   B. *poor* practice, since the shank part of the screw driver can be bent and the tool made useless
   C. *good* practice, since hammers and screw drivers are available in every tool kit just for this purpose
   D. *poor* practice, since the blade tip of the screw driver cannot be guided into the screw slot when both hands are holding the tools

18. Of the following, the reason why a tank, such as that pictured below, that is otherwise working correctly might fail to fill up sufficiently to deliver enough water to the toilet bowl at the time it is needed is that the   18._____

   A. ball may not drop back over the valve seat
   B. excess water may be flowing into the drain
   C. float rod may be bent up
   D. valve seat may be worn or nicked

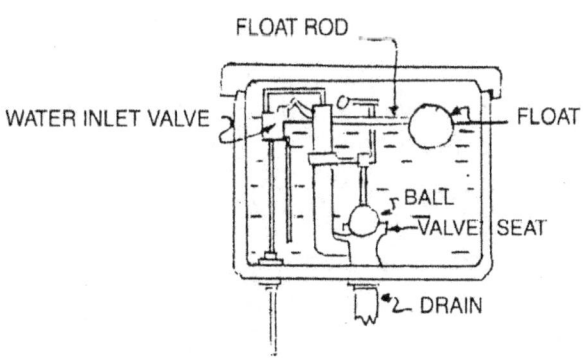

19. In the sketch below, the measurement of the inside diameter is *most nearly* _____ inches.   19.____

   A. 24　　　　B. 3　　　　C. 3 1/2　　　　D. 4

20. In a two-wire electrical system, the color of the wire which is grounded is *usually*   20.____

   A. white　　　　B. red　　　　C. black　　　　D. green

21. It is generally recommended that wooden ladders be kept coated with a suitable protective coating.   21.____
   The one of the following which is NOT a suitable protective coating is

   A. clear lacquer　　　　B. clear varnish
   C. linseed oil　　　　　　D. paint

22. The tool you should use to mend metal by soldering is   22.____

   A.　　　　B.　　　　C.　　　　D.

23. Of the following, the MOST effective method of fixing a door that sticks is to locate the area of the door which sticks and then to _____ it.   23.____

   A. lacquer　　　　B. plane　　　　C. tape　　　　D. varnish

24. Which one of the following should be used to thin latex paint?   24.____

   A. Mineral spirits　　　　B. Turpentine
   C. Denatured alcohol　　 D. Water

25. Of the following, the MAIN reason you should NOT place a ladder directly in front of a door that opens toward the ladder is that

    A. there is not enough space to support the weight of the ladder
    B. you would have to step down off the ladder each time someone wants to use the door
    C. this would prove to be hazardous if someone comes through the door
    D. it would be hard to reach the areas that need repair without tipping the ladder off balance

26. Going over the cutting line MORE than once when cutting a pane of glass by hand with a cutting wheel is *usually*

    A. *advisable;* it gives a straighter line
    B. *advisable;* it gives a cleaner break
    C. *inadvisable;* it gives an uneven break
    D. *inadvisable;* it may blunt the edge of the glass cutter

27. When hammering, it is usually BEST to hold the handle of the hammer

    A. close to the head because this maximizes the force of the blow
    B. far away from the head because this maximizes the force of the blow
    C. close to the head because this reduces the force of the blow
    D. far away from the head because this reduces the force of the blow

28. Repair crew members should report accidents on the job IMMEDIATELY *primarily* so that

    A. the proper person will be reprimanded for his carelessness
    B. a correct count can be kept of time lost through accidents
    C. prompt medical care may be given when needed
    D. the correct forms will be filled out

29. Leather gloves should be worn when handling sheet metal *primarily* because

    A. pressure on the metal might cause it to bend
    B. the edges and corners of the metal may be sharp
    C. natural oil or moisture from hands corrodes the metal
    D. leather provides a more secure grip

30. If a portable ladder does NOT have a nonslip base, the way to overcome this deficiency so that the ladder can be used safely is to

    A. place the ladder on soft earth
    B. fasten a wooden board across the top of the ladder
    C. splice two short ladders together
    D. tie the bottom of the ladder to a secure structure

KEY (CORRECT ANSWERS)

1.	C	16.	B
2.	A	17.	B
3.	B	18.	A
4.	D	19.	B
5.	D	20.	A
6.	D	21.	D
7.	B	22.	B
8.	C	23.	B
9.	C	24.	D
10.	A	25.	C
11.	C	26.	C
12.	D	27.	B
13.	B	28.	C
14.	B	29.	B
15.	D	30.	D

EXAMINATION SECTION
TEST 1

DIRECTIONS: Each question or incomplete statement is followed by several suggested answers or completions. Select the one that BEST answers the question or completes the statement. *PRINT THE LETTER OF THE CORRECT ANSWER IN THE SPACE AT THE RIGHT.*

1. As a member of a repair crew, you have been asked by your supervisor to reinforce a door. You have never done this kind of work before and are not certain how to go about it. Of the following, the MOST advisable action to take is to   1._____

    A. tell your supervisor you need assistance
    B. ask the other crew members if they can help you
    C. go ahead and do the best you can
    D. ask another member of your crew if he will do it for you

2. It is BEST to erect a barricade or barrier before repair work begins *mainly* because   2._____

    A. the repair truck can be sent back for additional supplies
    B. the workers can work in more comfortable space
    C. unauthorized persons are kept clear of the work area
    D. a solid platform is provided for workers' use

3. Of the following, the BEST reason for sprinkling water on work areas which have a lot of dust or where the work itself will create a lot of dust is that this action will   3._____

    A. dissolve the dust particles
    B. help the dust to settle
    C. clean away the dust from the area
    D. prevent the dust from drying out

QUESTIONS 4-9.
Questions 4 through 9 are to be answered *solely* on the basis of the following set of instructions.

Patching Simple Cracks in a Built-Up Roof

If there is a visible crack in built-up roofing, the repair is simple and straight forward:
1. With a brush, clean all loose gravel and dust out of the crack, and clean three or four inches around all sides of it.
2. With a trowel or putty knife, fill the crack with asphalt cement and then spread a layer of asphalt cement about 1/8 inch thick over the cleaned area.
3. Place a strip of roofing felt big enough to cover the crack into the wet cement and press it down firmly.
4. Spread a second layer of cement over the strip of felt and well past its edges.
5. Brush gravel back over the patch.

4. According to the above passage, in order to patch simple cracks in a built-up roof, it is necessary to use a   4._____

    A. putty knife and a drill   B. knife and pliers
    C. tack hammer and a punch   D. brush and a trowe

5. According to the above passage, the size of the area that should be clear of loose gravel and dust before the asphalt cement is first applied should

   A. be the exact size of the crack itself
   B. extend three or four inches on all sides of the crack
   C. be 1/8 inch greater than the size of the crack itself
   D. extend the length of the roofing strip

6. According to the above passage, loose gravel and dust in the crack should be removed with a

   A. brush   B. felt pad   C. trowel   D. dust mop

7. Assume that both layers of asphalt cement needed to patch the crack are of the same thickness.
   The total thickness of asphalt cement used in the patch should be, *most nearly*, _____ inch.

   A. 1/2   B. 1/3   C. 1/4   D. 1/8

8. According to the instructions in the above passage, how large should the strip of roofing felt be cut?

   A. Three of four inches square
   B. Smaller than the crack and small enough to be surrounded by cement on all sides of the strip
   C. Exactly the same size and shape of the area covered by the wet cement
   D. Large enough to completely cover the crack

9. The final or finishing action to be taken in patching a simple crack in a built-up roof is to

   A. clean out the inside of the crack
   B. spread a layer of asphalt a second time
   C. cover the crack with roofing felt
   D. cover the patch of roofing felt and cement with gravel

10. As a repair crew worker, your supervisor tells you that he has in the workshop a piece of glass measuring 5' x 4' from which he wants you to cut a section measuring 4'8" x 3'2". However, you find two pieces of glass in the workshop; one is 5' x 3', and the other is 8' x 5'.
    Of the following, the BEST action for you to take is to

    A. cut a section measuring 4'8" x 3' from the smaller piece because that is probably what he meant
    B. do NOT cut the glass and wait until he asks you for it
    C. tell him about the differences in measurement and ask him what to do
    D. cut a section measuring 4'8" x 3'2" from the larger piece since that would give you the full size required

11. A floor that is 9' wide by 12' long measures how many square feet?

    A. 12   B. 21   C. 108   D. 150

3 (#1)

12. The sum of 5 1/16, 4 1/4, 4 3/8, and 3 7/16 is   12.____

    A. 17 1/8   B. 17 7/16   C. 17 1/4   D. 17 3/8

13. From a length of pipe 6 feet 9 inches long you are asked to cut a piece 4 feet 5 inches   13.____
    long.
    The length of the remainder, in inches, should be

    A. 24   B. 26   C. 28   D. 53

QUESTIONS 14-17.
In answering questions 14 through 17 refer to the label pictured below.

LABEL

BREGSON'S CLEAR GLUE HIGHLY FLAMMABLE	PRECAUTIONS
A clear quick-drying glue	Use with adequate ventilation
For temporary bonding, apply glue to one surface and join immediately	Close container after use
For permanent bonding, apply glue to both surfaces, permit to dry and press together	Keep out of reach of children
Use for bonding plastic to plastic, plastic to wood, and wood to wood only	Avoid prolonged breathing of vapors and repeated contact with skin
Will not bond at temperatures below 60°	

14. Assume that you, as a member of a repair crew, have been asked to repair a wood ban-   14.____
    ister in the hallway of a house. Since the heat has been turned off, the hallway is very
    cold, except for the location where you have to make the repair. Another repair crew
    worker is working at that same location using a blow torch to solder a pipe in the wall.

    The temperature at that location is about 67°.
    According to the instruction on the above label, the use of this glue to make the neces-
    sary repair is

    A. *advisable;* the glue will bond wood to wood
    B. *advisable;* the heat form the soldering will cause the glue to dry quickly
    C. *inadvisable;* the work area temperature is too low
    D. *inadvisable;* the glue is highly flammable

15. According to the instructions on the above label, this glue should NOT be used for which   15.____
    of the following applications?

    A. Affixing a pine table leg to a walnut table
    B. Repairing leaks around pipe joints
    C. Bonding a plastic knob to a cedar drawer
    D. Attaching a lucite knob to a lucite drawer

16. According to the instructions on the above label, using this glue to bond ceramic tile to a plaster wall by coating both surfaces with glue, letting the glue dry, and then pressing the tile to the plaster wall is

    A. *advisable;* the glue is quick drying and clear
    B. *advisable;* the glue should be permanently affixed to the one surface of the tile only
    C. *inadvisable;* the glue is not suitable for bonding ceramic tile to plaster walls
    D. *inadvisable;* the bonding should be a temporary one

17. The precaution described in the above label "use with adequate ventilation" means that

    A. the area you are working in should be very cold
    B. there should be sufficient fresh air where you are using the glue
    C. you should wear gloves to avoid contact with the glue
    D. you must apply a lot of glue to make a permanent bond

QUESTIONS 18-20.
Questions 18 through 20 are to be answered *solely* on the basis of the following passage.

A utility plan is a floor plan which shows the layout of a heating, electrical, plumbing, or other utility system. Utility plans are used primarily by the persons responsible for the utilities, but they are important to the craftsman as well. Most utility installations require the leaving of openings in walls, floors, and roofs for the admission or installation of utility features. The craftsman who is, for example, pouring a concrete foundation wall must study the utility plans to determine the number, sizes, and locations of the openings he must leave for piping, electric lines, and the like.

18. The one of the following items of information which is LEAST likely to be provided by a utility plan is the

    A. location of the joists and frame members around
    B. stairwells
    C. location of the hot water supply and return piping
    D. location of light fixtures D. number of openings in the floor for radiators

19. According to the passage, the persons who will *most likely* have the GREATEST need for the information included in a utility plan of a building are those who

    A. maintain and repair the heating system
    B. clean the premises
    C. paint housing exteriors
    D. advertise property for sale

20. According to the passage, a repair crew member should find it MOST helpful to consult a utility plan when information is needed about the

    A. thickness of all doors in the structure
    B. number of electrical outlets located throughout the structure
    C. dimensions of each window in the structure
    D. length of a roof rafter

KEY (CORRECT ANSWERS)

1. A
2. C
3. B
4. D
5. B

6. A
7. C
8. D
9. D
10. C

11. C
12. A
13. C
14. D
15. B

16. C
17. B
18. A
19. A
20. B

TEST 2

DIRECTIONS: Each question or incomplete statement is followed by several suggested answers or completions. Select the one that BEST answers the question or completes the statement. *PRINT THE LETTER OF THE CORRECT ANSWER IN THE SPACE AT THE RIGHT.*

1. Repair crew men should report accidents on the job IMMEDIATELY *primarily* so that

   A. the proper person will be reprimanded for his carelessness
   B. a correct count can be kept of time lost through accidents on the job
   C. prompt medical care may be given when needed
   D. the correct forms will be filled out

2. In a circulating hot-water heating system, most boilers have an altitude gauge that shows the level of the water in the system. This gauge has two needles, one red, which is set at the proper water level, and one black, which shows the true water level, and which varies with the water-level change. When the red needle is over the black on the gauge, so that they coincide, it means that the system

   A. has too much water
   B. requires more water
   C. is properly filled with water
   D. should be shut off

3. If a radiator fails to heat properly, the FIRST of the following actions which you should take is to check the

   A. boiler's steam gauge
   B. boiler's water line
   C. radiator's shut-off valve
   D. pressure reducing valve

4. Assume that you have been asked to remove a door knob. You inspect the door and find that it has a mortise lock, and that the door knob is fastened with a set screw.
   Which of the following is the FIRST step that you should take in removing the door knob?

   A. Unscrew the set screw on the slimmest part of the knob
   B. Saw off the knob at its thinnest point
   C. Turn the knob repeatedly to the right and to the left until it finally falls off
   D. Use a pinchbar to spring the lock

5. When preparing a 1:1:6 mix for mortar, how many pails of lime should be added to 3 pails of sand and 1/2 pail of cement?

   A. 3   B. 1   C. 1/2   D. 1/4

6. If you find that the putty in the can is a little too hard to use, you should add some

   A. whiting
   B. linseed oil
   C. spackle
   D. glazing compound

7. The purpose of scratching the surface of the first coat of patching stucco is to   7.____

   A. spread the patching stucco over a wide area
   B. give the surface a textured finish
   C. provide a gripping surface for the next coat of patching stucco
   D. press the patching stucco into the hole to be repaired

8. When filling in large cracks and holes up to 2 inches in diameter in plaster walls it is BEST to use   8.____

   A. spackle   B. patching plaster
   C. gypsum wallboard   D. tile

9. Of the following, the MAIN reason for having a vertical distance of about 7 inches between stair treads is that this   9.____

   A. makes for the best appearance
   B. makes an easy step for the average person
   C. allows for the most profitable use of wood
   D. cuts out a good deal of unnecessary work

10. When removing a door from its hinges to make repairs, it is ALWAYS best to   10.____

    A. remove the pin from the top hinge first
    B. keep the door tightly closed
    C. remove the pin from the bottom hinge first
    D. remove the door knob and lock

11. Dry plaster will absorb water from the patching material, weakening and shrinking it. Based on the information in this statement, it would be *advisable* to take which one of the following actions in the process of patching a plaster crack?   11.____

    A. Mix the plaster with a lot of extra water
    B. Apply water-eased paint to the wall immediately
    C. Apply plaster powder to the crack, then pour water in over it
    D. Dampen the area surrounding the patch with a sponge

12. Standard electrical tools which are safe for ordinary use may be unsafe in locations which contain flammable materials because   12.____

    A. there may be insufficient ventilation
    B. sparks from the tools may start a fire
    C. electric current will usually cause fire
    D. the automatic sprinkler system may be set off accidentally

13. Of the following, the BEST combination of ingredients to use for good concrete is   13.____

    A. cement and water
    B. aggregate and water
    C. cement, sand, stone, and water
    D. gravel, cement, and water

14. If the blade of a screw driver is thicker than the slot at the top of a screw, the way to *properly* drive the screw into wood in this case is to

    A. widen the slot of the screw to fit the larger blade tip
    B. tap the end of the screw driver lightly to get a firmer hold into the screw slot
    C. get another screw driver which fits the size of the screw slot
    D. apply a drop of lubricating oil to the screw slot to get the screw started into the wood

QUESTIONS 15-20.
Questions 15 through 20 are to be answered *solely* on the basis of the following passage.

The basic hand-operated hoisting device is the tackle or purchase, consisting of a line called a fall, reeved through one or more blocks.

To hoist a load of given size, you must set up a rig with a safe working load equal to or in excess of the load to be hoisted. In order to do this, you must be able to calculate the safe working load of a single part of line of given size; the safe working load of a given purchase which contains a line of given size; and the minimum size of hooks or shackles which you must use in a given type of purchase to hoist a given load. You must also be able to calculate the thrust which a given load will exert on a gin pole or a set of shears inclined at a given angle; the safe working load which a spar of a given size, used as a gin pole or as one of a set of shears, will sustain; and the stress which a given load will set up in the back guy of a gin pole, or in the back guy of a set of shears, inclined at a given angle.

15. The above passage refers to the lifting of loads by means of

    A. erected scaffolds
    B. manual rigging devices
    C. power-driven equipment
    D. conveyor belts

16. It can be concluded from the above passage, that a set of shears serves to

    A. absorb the force and stress of the working load
    B. operate the tackle
    C. contain the working load
    D. compute the safe working load

17. According to the above passage, a spar can be used for a

    A. back guy   B. block   C. fall   D. gin pole

18. According to the above passage, the rule that a user of hand-operated tackle MUST follow is to make sure that the safe working load is at LEAST

    A. equal to the weight of the given load
    B. twice the combined weight of the block and falls
    C. one-half the weight of the given load
    D. twice the weight of the given load

19. According to the above passage, the two parts that make up a tackle are

    A. back guys and gin poles
    B. blocksm and falls
    C. rigs and shears
    D. spars and shackles

20. According to the above passage, in order to determine whether it is safe to hoist a particular load, you MUST

    A. use the maximum size hooks
    B. time the speed to bring a given load to a desired place
    C. calculate the forces exerted on various types of rigs
    D. repeatedly lift and lower various loads

20.____

KEY (CORRECT ANSWERS)

1.	C	11.	D
2.	C	12.	B
3.	C	13.	C
4.	A	14.	C
5.	C	15.	B
6.	B	16.	A
7.	C	17.	D
8.	B	18.	A
9.	B	19.	B
10.	C	20.	C

EXAMINATION SECTION
TEST 1

DIRECTIONS: Each question or incomplete statement is followed by several suggested answers or completions. Select the one that BEST answers the question or completes the statement. *PRINT THE LETTER OF THE CORRECT ANSWER IN THE SPACE AT THE RIGHT.*

1. Asbestos was used as a covering on electrical wires to provide protection from

    A. high voltage
    B. high temperature
    C. water damage
    D. electrolysis

2. The rating term *240 volts, 10 H.P.* would be PROPERLY used to describe a

    A. transformer
    B. storage battery
    C. motor
    D. rectifier

3. Rigid steel conduit used for the protection of electrical wiring is GENERALLY either galvanized or enameled both inside and out in order to

    A. prevent damage to the wire insulation
    B. make threading of the conduit easier
    C. prevent corrosion of the conduit
    D. make the conduit easier to handle

4. BX is COMMONLY used to indicate

    A. rigid conduit without wires
    B. flexible conduit without wires
    C. insulated wires covered with flexible steel armor
    D. insulated wires covered with a non-metallic covering

5. If a test lamp does not light when placed in series with a fuse and an appropriate battery, it is a GOOD indication that the fuse

    A. is open-circuited
    B. is short-circuited
    C. is in operating condition
    D. has zero resistance

6. Of the following, the SIMPLEST wood joint to make is a

    A. half lap joint
    B. mortise and tenon
    C. butt joint
    D. multiple dovetail

7. To accurately cut a number of lengths of wood at an angle of 45 degrees, it would be BEST to use a

    A. protractor
    B. mitre-box
    C. triangle
    D. square

8. The soffit of a beam is the

    A. span
    B. side
    C. bottom
    D. top

9. A nail set is a tool used for

   A. straightening bent nails
   B. cutting nails to specified size
   C. sinking a nail head in wood
   D. measuring nail size

10. It is UNLAWFUL to

    A. use wooden lath
    B. have ceiling lath run in one direction only
    C. break joints when using wood lath
    D. run wood lath through from room to room

11. A concrete mix for a construction job requires a certain ratio of cement, water, sand, and small stones.
    The MOST serious error in mixing would be to use 20% too much

    A. sand
    B. water
    C. small stones
    D. mixing time

12. Impurities in a mortar which may seriously affect its strength are MOST likely to enter the mortar with the

    A. mixing water
    B. sand
    C. lime
    D. gypsum

13. One ADVANTAGE of using plywood instead of boards for concrete forms is that plywood

    A. needs no bracing
    B. does not split easily
    C. sticks less to concrete
    D. insulates concrete against freezing

14. Concrete will crack MOST easily when it is subject to

    A. compression
    B. bearing
    C. bonding
    D. tension

15. Where a smooth dense finish is desired for a concrete surface, it will BEST be produced by using a

    A. wood float
    B. level
    C. steel trowel
    D. vibrator

16. Sewer gas is prevented from backing up through a fixture by a

    A. water trap
    B. vent pipe
    C. check valve
    D. float valve

17. Packing is used in an adjustable water valve MAINLY to

    A. make it air-tight
    B. prevent mechanical wear
    C. regulate the water pressure
    D. make it water-tight

18. Good practice requires that the end of a piece of water pipe be reamed to remove the inside burr after it has been cut to length.
The PURPOSE of the reaming is to

    A. finish the pipe accurately to length
    B. make the threading easier
    C. avoid cutting of the workers' hands
    D. allow free passage for the flow of water

19. The MAIN reason for pitching a steam pipe in a heating system is to

    A. prevent accumulation of condensed steam
    B. present a smaller radiating surface
    C. facilitate repairs
    D. reduce friction in the pipe

20. When fitting pipe together, poor alignment of pipe and fittings would MOST likely result in

    A. leaky joints
    B. cracking of the pipe on expansion
    C. formation of hot spots
    D. cracking of the pipe on contraction

21. Roofing nails are GENERALLY

    A. brass plated   B. galvanized
    C. cement coated   D. nickel plated

22. Specifications for a roofing job call for 3 *lbs. sheet lead*. This means that each sheet SHOULD weigh 3 lbs. per

    A. square inch   B. square foot
    C. square yard   D. sheet

23. The MAIN reason for using flashing at the intersection of different roof planes is to

    A. increase the durability of the shingles
    B. simplify the installation of the shingles
    C. waterproof the roof
    D. improve the appearance of the roof

24. Of the following roofing materials, the one that is MOST frequently used in *built-up* roofs is

    A. asbestos shingles   B. three-ply felt
    C. sheet copper   D. wood sheathing

25. As used in roofing, *a square* refers to

    A. a tool for lining up the roofing with the eaves of the house
    B. one hundred square feet of roofing
    C. one hundred shingles of roofing
    D. one hundred pounds of roofing

26. In the process of replacing a pane of window glass, the old putty should be scraped off the window sash and the wood surfaces then primed with

    A. resin oil
    B. shellac
    C. linseed oil
    D. enamel

26._____

27. The LARGEST available size of glazier's points is number

    A. 3   B. 1   C. 0   D. 000

27._____

28. The purpose of priming wood window sash before applying putty and glass is to prevent the

    A. putty from absorbing moisture from the wood
    B. putty from staining the wood
    C. wood from absorbing the oils from the putty
    D. natural wood resins from making the putty brittle

28._____

29. When hard, dry putty must be removed from a wood window frame in order to put in a new pane of glass, the BEST tool with which to do this job is a

    A. screwdriver
    B. putty knife
    C. wide wood chisel
    D. pocket knife

29._____

30. Before repainting a wood surface on which the old paint film has developed some wrinkling, the MOST appropriate treatment for the wood surface is a

    A. thorough scraping
    B. light shellacking
    C. wash-down with dilute muriatic acid
    D. rubbing down of the wrinkles with fairly coarse sand-paper

30._____

31. A paint that is characterized by its ability to dry to an especially smooth, hard, glossy or semi-glossy finish is called a(n)

    A. primer   B. sealer   C. glaze   D. enamel

31._____

32. The BEST thinner for varnish is

    A. gasoline
    B. turpentine
    C. kerosene
    D. water

32._____

33. To get a good paint job on a new plaster wall, one should make certain that the

    A. wall is thoroughly dry before painting
    B. base coat is much darker than the finishing coat
    C. wall has been roughened enough to make the paint stick
    D. plaster has not completely set

33._____

34. In a three-coat plaster job, the brown coat is applied

    A. before the scratch coat has set
    B. immediately after the scratch coat
    C. after the scratch coat has set and partially dried
    D. after the scratch coat has thoroughly dried out

34._____

35. Plaster which has sand as an aggregate, when compared with plaster which has a light-weight aggregate, is

    A. a better sound absorber
    B. a better insulator
    C. less likely to crack under a sharp blow
    D. cheaper

36. One form of metal lath comes in sheets 27" x 96".
    The number of sheets required to cover 20 square yards without overlap is

    A. 9 B. 10 C. 11 D. 12

37. When nailing gypsum board lath to studs or furring strips, the nailing should be started_____ of the board.

    A. along the top   B. along the bottom
    C. at the center   D. at one end

38. A wooden mortar box for slaking lime is lined with sheet iron.
    Of the following, the GREATEST advantage of the lining is that

    A. a better grade putty is produced
    B. the box is easier to clean
    C. it makes the box water-tight
    D. it prevents burning of the wood

39. The Building Code requires that water used in plastering MUST

    A. be perfectly clear in color
    B. not have any rust in it
    C. be fit for drinking
    D. not be fluoridated

40. In order to prevent thin sheet metal from buckling when riveting it to an angle iron, the BEST procedure is to

    A. start riveting at one end of the sheet and work toward the other end
    B. start riveting at both ends of the sheet and work in toward the center
    C. install alternate rivets working in one direction, and then fill in the remaining rivets working in the other direction
    D. start riveting in the center of the joint, working out in both directions

KEY (CORRECT ANSWERS)

1. B	11. B	21. B	31. D
2. C	12. B	22. B	32. B
3. C	13. B	23. C	33. A
4. C	14. D	24. B	34. C
5. A	15. C	25. B	35. D
6. C	16. A	26. C	36. B
7. B	17. D	27. C	37. C
8. C	18. D	28. C	38. B
9. C	19. A	29. C	39. C
10. D	20. A	30. D	40. D

TEST 2

DIRECTIONS: Each question or incomplete statement is followed by several suggested answers or completions. Select the one that BEST answers the question or completes the statement. *PRINT THE LETTER OF THE CORRECT ANSWER IN THE SPACE AT THE RIGHT.*

1. A drill bit measures .625 inches.
   The FRACTIONAL EQUIVALENT, in inches, is

   A. 9/16   B. 5/8   C. 11/16   D. 3/4

2. The number of cubic yards of sand required to fill a bin measuring 12 feet by 6 feet by 4 feet is MOST NEARLY

   A. 8   B. 11   C. 48   D. 96

3. Assume that you are assigned to put down floor tiles in a room measuring 8 feet by 10 feet. Individual tiles measure 9 inches by 9 inches.
   The total number of floor tiles required to cover the entire floor is MOST NEARLY

   A. 107   B. 121   C. 144   D. 160

4. Lumber is usually sold by the board foot, and a board foot is defined as a board one foot square and one inch thick.
   If the price of one board foot of lumber is 18 cents and you need 20 feet of lumber 6 inches wide and 1 inch thick, the cost of the 20 feet of the lumber is

   A. $1.80   B. $2.40   C. $3.60   D. $4.80

5. For a certain plumbing repair job, you need three lengths of pipe, 12 1/4 inches, 6 1/2 inches, and 8 5/8 inches.
   If you cut these three lengths from the same piece of pipe, which is 36 inches long, and each cut consumes 1/8 inch of pipe, the length of pipe REMAINING after you have cut out your three pieces should be _____ inches.

   A. 7 1/4   B. 7 7/8   C. 8 1/4   D. 8 7/8

6. Glazier points are small pieces of galvanized metal often having the shape of a(n)

   A. circle   B. ellipse   C. square   D. triangle

7. Putty that is too stiff is made workable by adding

   A. gasoline   B. linseed oil
   C. water   D. lacquer thinner

8. Soap is applied to wood screws before they are used in order to

   A. prevent rust
   B. make a tight fit
   C. make insertion easier
   D. prevent screws from loosening after insertion

9. A method sometimes used to prevent a pipe from buckling during a bending operation is to

A. bend the pipe very quickly
B. keep the seam of the pipe on the outside of the bend
C. nick the pipe at the center of the bend
D. pack the inside of the pipe with sand

10. Rubber gaskets are frequently placed between the faces of the flanges when making up a flanged joint in a pipe line in order to

   A. prevent corrosion of the machined faces
   B. permit full tightening of the flange bolts without danger of thread stripping
   C. eliminate the necessity for accurate alignment of the pipe
   D. make a tight joint

11. A parapet is the

   A. stepping out of successive courses of brickwork
   B. continuation of a wall above the roof line
   C. wall enclosing stairs that lead to the roof
   D. portion of an exterior wall below a window

12. The process of removing the insulation from a wire is called

   A. braiding   B. skinning   C. sweating   D. tinning

13. The process of making fresh concrete watertight, durable, and strong after it has been poured is called

   A. air-entraining   B. finishing
   C. curing   D. accelerating

14. A mixture of cement, sand, and water is called

   A. hydrated lime   B. plain concrete
   C. hydrated cement   D. mortar

15. The *grip* applied to a pipe with gas pliers is increased by using pliers with

   A. longer handles   B. larger jaws
   C. thicker handles   D. larger teeth

16. Those materials which are added to a paint vehicle to regulate its consistency and thus increase its spreading power and facilitate its application are called

   A. driers   B. thinners
   C. extenders   D. oxidents

17. The fitting which usually is easiest to disconnect FIRST when disassembling a piping run is a(n)

   A. cross   B. union
   C. return bend   D. elbow

18. For convenience in case of future repairs to a long pipe line, it is DESIRABLE to fit the pipe together with several

   A. street ells   B. elbows
   C. return bends   D. unions

19. If four pipes are to be connected into each other at a common point, it would be NECESSARY to use a(n)

    A. tee fitting B. street ell
    C. cross D. offset

20. The BEST of the following tools to use for cutting off a piece of single conductor #6 rubber insulated lead covered cable is a

    A. pair of electrician's pliers
    B. hacksaw
    C. hammer and cold chisel
    D. lead knife

21. One ADVANTAGE of rubber insulation is that it

    A. does not deteriorate with age
    B. is able to withstand high temperature
    C. does not absorb much moisture
    D. is not damaged by oil

22. The SIMPLEST device for interrupting an overloaded electrical circuit is a

    A. fuse B. relay
    C. capacitor D. choke-coil

23. Reinforced concrete USUALLY means concrete that has been strengthened by use of

    A. additional cement B. steel bars
    C. extra heavy gravel D. high strength cement

24. A VERTICAL wood member in the wall of a wood frame house is known as a

    A. stringer B. ridge member
    C. stud D. header

25. A riser is GENERALLY a pipe run which is

    A. horizontal B. curved
    C. vertical D. at a 45-degree angle

26. A standard pipe thread DIFFERS from a standard screw thread in that the pipe thread

    A. is tapered
    B. is deeper
    C. requires no lubrication when cutting
    D. has the same pitch for any diameter of pipe

27. The material which is LEAST likely to be found in use as the outer covering of rubber insulated wires or cables is

    A. cotton B. varnished cambric
    C. lead D. neoprene

28. In measuring to determine the size of a standard insulated conductor, the PROPER place to use the wire gauge is on

A. the insulation
B. the outer covering
C. the stranded conductor
D. one strand of the conductor

29. Rubber insulation on an electrical conductor would MOST quickly be damaged by continuous contact with

   A. acid B. water C. oil D. alkali

30. If a fuse clip becomes hot under normal circuit load, the MOST probable cause is that the

   A. clip makes poor contact with the fuse ferrule
   B. circuit wires are too small
   C. current rating of the fuse is too high
   D. voltage rating of the fuse is too low

31. If the input to a 10 to 1 step-down transformer is 15 amperes at 2400 volts, the secondary output would be NEAREST to _____ amperes at _____ volts.

   A. 1.5; 24,000
   B. 150; 240
   C. 1.5; 240
   D. 150; 24,000

32. The resistance of a copper wire to the flow of electricity _____ as the _____ of the wire _____.

   A. increases; diameter; increases
   B. decreases; diameter; decreases
   C. decreases; length; increases
   D. increases; length; increases

33. Where galvanized steel conduit is used, the PRIMARY purpose of the galvanizing is to

   A. increase mechanical strength
   B. retard rusting
   C. provide a good surface for painting
   D. provide good electrical contact for grounding

34. The lamps used for station and tunnel lighting in the subways are generally operated at slightly less than their rated voltage.
The LOGICAL reason for this is to

   A. prevent overloading of circuits
   B. increase the life of the lamps
   C. decrease glare
   D. obtain a more even distribution of light

35. The CORRECT method of measuring the power taken by an a.c. electric motor is to use a

   A. wattmeter
   B. voltmeter and an ammeter
   C. power factor meter
   D. tachometer

36. Wood ladders should NOT be painted because the paint   36.____

    A. may deteriorate the wood
    B. makes the ladders slippery
    C. is inflammable
    D. may cover cracks or defects

37. Goggles would be LEAST necessary when   37.____

    A. recharging soda-acid fire extinguishers
    B. chipping stone
    C. putting electrolyte into an Edison battery
    D. scraping rubber insulation from a wire

38. The number and type of precautions to be taken on a job generally depend LEAST on the   38.____

    A. nature of the job
    B. length of time the job is expected to last
    C. kind of tools and materials being used
    D. location of the work

39. When training workers in the use of tools and equipment, safety precautions related to their use should be FIRST mentioned   39.____

    A. in the introductory training session before the workers begin to use the equipment or tools
    B. during training sessions when workers practice operating the tools or equipment
    C. after the workers are qualified to use the equipment in their daily tasks
    D. when an agency safety bulletin related to the tools and equipment is received

40. Many portable electric power tools, such as electric drills, have a third conductor in the power lead which is used to connect the case of the tool to a grounded part of the electric outlet.   40.____
    The reason for this extra conductor is to

    A. have a spare wire in case one power wire should break
    B. strengthen the power lead so it cannot easily be damaged
    C. prevent the user of the tool from being shocked
    D. enable the tool to be used for long periods of time without overheating

KEY (CORRECT ANSWERS)

1. B	11. B	21. C	31. B
2. B	12. B	22. A	32. D
3. C	13. C	23. B	33. B
4. A	14. D	24. C	34. B
5. C	15. A	25. C	35. A
6. D	16. B	26. A	36. D
7. B	17. B	27. B	37. D
8. C	18. D	28. D	38. B
9. D	19. C	29. C	39. A
10. D	20. B	30. A	40. C

EXAMINATION SECTION
TEST 1

DIRECTIONS: Each question or incomplete statement is followed by several suggested answers or completions. Select the one that BEST answers the question or completes the statement. *PRINT THE LETTER OF THE CORRECT ANSWER IN THE SPACE AT THE RIGHT.*

1. A shrink fitted collar is to be removed from a shaft. One good way to do this would be to drive out the shaft after _____ collar. 1.____

    A. *chilling* only the
    B. *chilling* both the shaft and
    C. *heating* only the
    D. *heating* both the shaft and

2. It is CORRECT to say that 2.____

    A. a standard brick weighs about 8 lbs.
    B. the dimensions of a common brick are 8" x 3 3/4" x 2 1/4"
    C. vertical joints in a brick wall are called bed joints
    D. in laying bricks the head joints should be slushed with mortar

3. A snail pump impeller is checked for static balance by 3.____

    A. running the pump at high speed and listening for rubs
    B. mounting it on parallel and level knife edges and noting if it turns
    C. weighing it and comparing the weight against the original weight
    D. putting it on a lathe to see if it runs true

4. The sum of the following dimensions: 3' x 2 1/4", 8 7/8", 2'6 3/8", 2'9 3/4", and 1'0" is 4.____

    A. 16'7 1/4"   B. 10'7 1/4"   C. 10'3 1/4"   D. 9'3 1/4"

5. A requisition for nails was worded as follows: *100 lbs., 10d, 3 inch, common wive nails, galvanized.*
The UNNECESSARY information in this requisition is 5.____

    A. 100 lbs.   B. common   C. galvanized   D. 3 inch

6. Electric arc welding is COMMONLY done by the use of _____ voltage and _____ amperage. 6.____

    A. *low; high*   B. *high; high*
    C. *high; low*   D. *low; low*

7. A GOOD principle for you to follow after teaching a maintenance procedure to a new helper is to 7.____

    A. tell him that you expect him to make many mistakes at first
    B. observe his work procedure and point out any errors he may make
    C. have him write out the procedure from memory
    D. assume he knows the procedure if he asks no questions

8. Multiple threads are used on the stems of some large valves to

   A. reduce the effort required to open the valve
   B. prevent binding of the valve stem
   C. secure faster opening and closing of the valve
   D. decrease the length of stem travel

9. After the base plate of a new machine has been fitted over the foundation bolts, it should be leveled by

   A. inserting steel shims under the plate
   B. chipping the high spots off the floor
   C. using thin cement grout under the plate
   D. grinding down the high spots on the base plate

10. In nixing concrete by hand, the materials are first thoroughly mixed dry and then mixed with water. This is a good procedure because it

    A. caves cement
    B. reduces the amount of water required
    C. avoids settling of the aggregate
    D. properly coats the aggregate with the cement

11. A revolution counter applied to the end of a rotating shaft reads 100 when a stopwatch is started and 850 after 90 seconds.
    The shaft is rotating at a speed of _____ rpm.

    A. 500   B. 633   C. 750   D. 950

12. If a kink develops in a wire rope, it would be BEST to

    A. hammer out the kink with a lead hammer
    B. straighten out the kink by putting it in a vise and applying sufficient pressure
    C. discard the portion of the rope containing the kink
    D. keep the rope in use and allow the kink to work itself out

13. Steel pipe posts have been placed into prepared holes in concrete.
    To properly secure the posts, they should be caulked inplace with

    A. molten lead   B. cement mortar
    C. oakum   D. hot pitch

14. The PRINCIPAL reason for grounding of electrical equipment is to

    A. save power   B. guard against shock
    C. prevent open circuits   D. prevent short circuits

15. A spirit level has been dropped and a deep indentation made in the wood.
    The BEST thing to do is to

    A. ignore the incident if the bubbles were not broken
    B. sand down the surface to remove the indentation
    C. get a new level
    D. test the level

16. A strike plate is MOST closely associated with a 16.____

   A. lock B. sash weight
   C. hinge D. door check

17. You receive a special assignment from your superior calling for the use of a type of wood 17.____
   which in your opinion is not suitable for the job.
   You should

   A. substitute the wood you believe to be most suitable
   B. carry out the order as received
   C. immediately call this to his attention
   D. consult another maintainer on what to do

18. A motor driven centrifugal pump takes water from a city main and delivers it to the noz- 18.____
   zles of a train washing machine. With little change in motor speed or suction pressure,
   the discharge pressure rises and the flow of cleaning water falls to a trickle.
   The PROBABLE cause is a

   A. failure of the impeller shaft
   B. leak in the piping between the pressure gage point of attachment and the nozzles
   C. blockage of the impeller
   D. blockage between the pressure gage point of attachment and the nozzles

19. A standard hoisting rope size is designated as 6 x 19. This indicates that the rope has 19.____

   A. 6 strands, each made of 19 wires
   B. 19 strands, each made of 6 wires
   C. 6 strands of No. 19 gage wire
   D. 19 strands of No. 6 gage wire

20. The two planes which make up the MOST useful combination 20.____
   for general carpentry work are the _____ plane and the _____ plane.

   A. jack; jointer B. jack; block
   C. smooth; block D. fore; jointer

21. If you were drilling a structural plate and the drill cuttings were in the form of long contin- 21.____
   uous shavings, you could rightly conclude that the

   A. drill point was too sharp
   B. material being drilled was wrought iron
   C. bearing pressure on the drill was insufficient
   D. drilling was being done correctly

22. Studs and joists for light building construction are USUALLY spaced on _____ inch cen- 22.____
   ters.

   A. 12 B. 14 C. 16 D. 18

23. If power driven rivets are loose, the MOST likely reason would be that the rivets were 23.____

   A. too long
   B. too short
   C. driven with high air pressure
   D. overheated

24. If a drawing for a pipe installation is made to a scale of 1 1/2" to the foot, the drawing is said to be one _____ size.

    A. half   B. quarter   C. eighth   D. sixteenth

25. A gear train consists of a driver with 120 teeth, an idler with 60 teeth, and a driven gear with 200 teeth. If the driver rotates at 1500 rpm, the driven gear rotates at _____ rpm.

    A. 225   B. 900   C. 2500   D. 10,000

26. A certain pipe fitting is marked *200 WOG*. This fitting could NOT properly be used in a pipe line for _____ pounds gage maximum.

    A. steam at 200   B. water at 150
    C. air at 200   D. oil at 150

27. A file having two *safe* edges is COMMONLY known as a _____ file.

    A. flat   B. mill   C. hand   D. pillar

28. By trial, it is found that by using 2 cubic feet of sand, a 5 cubic foot batch of concrete is produced.
    Using the same proportions, the amount of sand, in cubic feet, required to produce 2 cubic yards of concrete is MOST NEARLY

    A. 7   B. 22   C. 27   D. 45

29. Tooling of the face joints of a brick wall under construction should be done

    A. after the mortar has acquired its initial set
    B. after the entire wall is laid
    C. after the mortar has acquired its final set
    D. as each brick is laid

30. A gland bushing is associated in practice with a(n)

    A. gas engine   B. electric motor
    C. centrifugal pump   D. lathe

31. A house drain is successively offset by means of a 1/8 bend, a 1/16 bend, and a 1/32 bend.
    The total angular offset of this line is MOST NEARLY

    A. 34°   B. 39°   C. 68°   D. 79°

32. The flushing mechanism in a low tank water closet is so arranged that a fill tube supplies water from the ball cock to the overflow standpipe for a short interval immediately after the closet is flushed.
    The MAIN reason for this is to

    A. finish cleaning the water passages of the closet
    B. properly seal the ball in its seat
    C. renew the seal in the closet trap
    D. scour the flush tube from the tank to the closet

33. A job calls for the setting of wrought iron pipe sleeves in concrete floor construction for the passage of water risers.
    In order to provide for the passage of a 2" riser, the MINIMUM diameter of the sleeve is

    A. 2 1/2"   B. 3"   C. 4"   D. 5"

34. When applied to lumber, the designation *S4S* means

    A. all sides are rough
    B. all four sides are of the same size
    C. fourth grade lumber
    D. all sides are dressed

35. To guard against accidents in connection with wood scaffolding,

    A. inspect the nailing before the scaffold is loaded
    B. never put a heavy load on a scaffold
    C. use only heavy timber for scaffold construction
    D. do not build high scaffolds

36. A reducing tee has one run opening of 2 inches, the second run opening of 14 inches, and the branch opening of 1 inch.
    This tee would be specified as

    A. 1 x 1 1/2 x 2   B. 1 x 2 x 1 1/2
    C. 2 x 1 1/2 x 1   D. 2 x 1 x 1 1/2

37. A length of pipe is to be fitted with a 90° elbow at each end. The center to center distance between elbows is to be 4'6". The center to end dimension of each elbow is 2" and the thread engagement is 1/2".
    The length to which the pipe should be cut is

    A. 4'1"   B. 4'2"   C. 4'3"   D. 4'4 1/2"

38. Sheet metal seams are sometimes grooved. The MAIN function of the grooving is to

    A. facilitate making a soldered joint
    B. prevent unlocking
    C. improve the appearance of the joint
    D. save sheet metal

39. When fitting new piston rings in a compressor, the piston ring gap is BEST measured by means of a(n)

    A. feeler gage   B. inside caliper
    C. 6" rule   D. depth gage

40. The ampere-hour rating of a battery depends MAINLY on the

    A. number of cells connected in series
    B. casing composition
    C. quantity of electrolyte
    D. number and area of the battery plates

KEY (CORRECT ANSWERS)

1. C	11. A	21. D	31. D
2. B	12. C	22. C	32. C
3. B	13. A	23. B	33. B
4. C	14. B	24. C	34. D
5. D	15. D	25. B	35. A
6. A	16. A	26. A	36. C
7. B	17. C	27. D	37. C
8. C	18. D	28. B	38. B
9. A	19. A	29. A	39. A
10. D	20. B	30. C	40. D

TEST 2

DIRECTIONS: Each question or incomplete statement is followed by several suggested answers or completions. Select the one that BEST answers the question or completes the statement. *PRINT THE LETTER OF THE CORRECT ANSWER IN THE SPACE AT THE RIGHT.*

1. In making a high wooden scaffold, proper splices in 2 x 4 lumber which is to be used vertically would be made by

   A. lapping each joint with a cleat below
   B. butting the ends and boxing in the joints with 1" boards
   C. butting the ends and nailing a 2 x 4 over the splice
   D. making half-lap joints

   1.____

2. With respect to soldering, it is LEAST important that

   A. the soldering copper be clean and well-tinned
   B. a good flux suitable for the metal being soldered be used
   C. the joint to be soldered be well-cleaned
   D. a lot of solder be used

   2.____

3. When two sheet metal plates are riveted together, a specified minimum distance must be provided from the edge of each plate to the nearest line of rivets in order to prevent

   A. the rivet heads from working loose
   B. the rivets from being sheared
   C. tearing of the material between the rivets and the edges of the plates
   D. excessive stress on the rivets

   3.____

4. A hoisting cable is wound on a 14" drum which is rotating at 5 rpm. The load being raised by this cable will move at an APPROXIMATE linear speed, in feet per minute, of

   A. 13.5   B. 18.3   C. 70   D. 220

   4.____

5. Spreaders are used in connection with forms for concrete to

   A. hold the walls of a form the correct distance apart
   B. anchor a form to the ground
   C. make a form watertight
   D. make the cement spread evenly through the form

   5.____

6. By curing of concrete is meant

   A. finishing the surface of the concrete
   B. softening stiff concrete by adding water
   C. keeping the concrete wet while setting
   D. the salvaging of frozen concrete

   6.____

7. If steel weighs 480 lbs. per cubic foot, the weight of an 18" x 18" x 2" steel base plate is _____ lbs.

   A. 180   B. 216   C. 427   D. 648

   7.____

8. Standard wrought iron pipe and extra strong wrought iron pipe of the same nominal size differ in

   A. outside diameter
   B. inside diameter
   C. chemical composition
   D. threading

9. Plumbing system stacks are vented to the atmosphere. These stacks will NOT

   A. relieve the back pressure on traps from the sewer side
   B. prevent the siphoning of traps
   C. ventilate the drainage system
   D. prevent the sewer from backing up into the fixtures

10. The MOST likely cause of accidents involving minor injuries is

    A. careless work practices
    B. lack of safety devices
    C. inferior equipment and material
    D. insufficient safety posters

11. In the maintenance of shop equipment, lubrication should be done

    A. periodically
    B. only if necessary
    C. whenever time permits
    D. only during the overhaul period

12. The total number of cubic yards of earth to be removed to nake a trench 3'9" wide, 25'0" long, and 4'3" deep is MOST NEARLY

    A. 53.1   B. 35.4   C. 26.6   D. 11.8

13. A large number of 2 x 4 studs, some 10'5" long and some 6'5 1/2" long, are required for a job.
    To minimize waste, it would be preferable to order lengths of _____ ft.

    A. 16   B. 17   C. 18   D. 19

14. A 6" pipe is connected to a 4" pipe through a reducer. If 100 cubic feet of water is flowing through the 6" pipe per minute, the flow, in cubic feet per minute, through the 4" pipe is

    A. 225   B. 100   C. 66.6   D. 44.4

15. The type of seam generally used in the construction of sheet metal cylinders of small diameters is the _____ seam.

    A. double edged
    B. folded
    C. double hemmed
    D. simple lap

16. Two branch ventilating ducts, one 12 inches square and the other 18 inches square, are to connect to a square main duct.
    In order to maintain the same cross-sectional area, the dimension of the main duct should be _____ inches square.

    A. 14   B. 20   C. 24   D. 28

17. In reference to preparing mortar, it is CORRECT to say that the lime used

   A. may burn the skin
   B. hastens setting
   C. prevents absorption of water by the brick
   D. decreases the amount of water needed

18. The intercooler of a two-stage air compressor is connected to the compressor unit

   A. before the air intake pipe to the first stage
   B. between the second stage and the receiver
   C. between the two stages
   D. after the receiver.

19. In oxyacetylene welding, the hose that is connected to the oxygen cylinder is USUALLY colored

   A. yellow   B. white   C. purple   D. green

20. When bonding new concrete to old concrete, the surface of the old concrete should be

   A. left untouched   B. dry
   C. carefully smoothed   D. chipped and roughened

21. A sack of Portland cement is considered to have a volume, in cubic feet, of

   A. 1/2   B. 3/4   C. 1   D. 14

22. The purpose of a vacuum breaker used with an automatic flush valve is to

   A. limit the flow of water to the fixture
   B. prevent pollution of the water supply
   C. equalize the water pressure
   D. control the water pressure to the fixture

23. Wiping solder for lead pipe USUALLY has a melting range of _____ °F.

   A. 150 to 250   B. 251 to 350
   C. 360 to 470   D. 475 to 600

24. A space heater is to be suspended from a structural beam. The heater should be suspended by a hanger

   A. passing through a hole in the web of the beam
   B. passing through a hole in the flange of the beam
   C. welded to the beam
   D. clamped to the beam

25. With respect to babbitted sleeve bearings, oil grooves are

   A. cut only on the top half
   B. cut only on the bottom half
   C. cut on both halves
   D. never necessary

26. When an employee finds it necessary to work near a live third rail, it is BEST to cover the third rail with a

    A. rubber mat
    B. canvas cloth
    C. board
    D. sheet of heavy paper

27. A 10-inch foundation wall is 11 feet long and 15 feet high. If the compressive strength of the wall is 300 pounds per square inch, the MAXIMUM permissible load on this wall is _____ lbs.

    A. 540,000   B. 495,000   C. 396,000   D. 33,000

28. It is INCORRECT to state that

    A. neat cement contains cement and water
    B. salt is used to hasten the setting of concrete
    C. the strength of concrete is affected by the water ratio
    D. a sidewalk should slope toward the street

29. When sharpening a hand saw, the FIRST operation is to file the teeth so that they are of the same height. This is known as

    A. shaping   B. setting   C. leveling   D. jointing

30. The swing of a lathe is the

    A. diameter of the largest piece that can be turned
    B. distance between centers of the head and tail spindles
    C. size of the face plate
    D. radius of the chuck

31. Assume that the lead screw, stud gear, and spindle of a lathe revolve at the same speed. It is required to cut 10 threads per inch when the lead screw has 6 threads per inch. If the stud gear has 48 teeth, the lead screw gear must have _____ teeth.

    A. 48   B. 60   C. 64   D. 80

32. The safety device used on a crane to prevent overtravel is called a(n)

    A. unloader
    B. governor
    C. limit switch
    D. overload relay

33. It is INCORRECT to say that

    A. there is a difference between fittings for threaded drainage pipe and fittings for ordinary threaded pipe
    B. a gasoline torch must be fully filled with gasoline
    C. *Red Brass* pipe contains about 85% copper
    D. loose parts in a faucet may cause noisy operation

34. A requisition for lag screws does NOT require stating the

    A. diameter
    B. quantity
    C. threads per inch
    D. length

35. In an accident report, the information which may be MOST useful in decreasing the recurrence of similar type accidents is the

    A. extent of injuries sustained
    B. time the accident happened
    C. number of people involved
    D. cause of the accident

36. Carbon tetrachloride is NOT recommended for cleaning purposes because of

    A. the poisonous nature of its fumes
    B. its limited cleaning value
    C. the damaging effects it has on equipment
    D. the difficulty of application

37. The part of the thread directly measured with a thread micrometer is the

    A. thread height
    B. major diameter
    C. thread lead
    D. pitch diameter

38. The side support for steps or stairs is called a

    A. ledger board
    B. runner
    C. stringer
    D. riser

39. A sheet metal plate has been cut in the form of a right triangle with sides of 5, 12, and 13 inches.
    The area of this plate, in square inches, is

    A. 30   B. 32 1/2   C. 60   D. 78

40. The BEST first aid for a man who has no external injury but is apparently suffering from internal injury due to an accident is to

    A. take him at once to a doctor's office
    B. make him comfortable and immediately summon a doctor or ambulance
    C. administer a stimulant
    D. start artificial respiration

KEY (CORRECT ANSWERS)

1. B	11. A	21. C	31. D
2. D	12. D	22. B	32. C
3. C	13. C	23. C	33. B
4. B	14. B	24. D	34. C
5. A	15. D	25. A	35. D
6. C	16. B	26. A	36. A
7. A	17. A	27. C	37. D
8. B	18. C	28. B	38. C
9. D	19. D	29. D	39. A
10. A	20. D	30. A	40. B

SAFETY EXAMINATION SECTION
TEST 1

DIRECTIONS: Each question or incomplete statement is followed by several suggested answers or completions. Select the one that BEST answers the question or completes the statement. *PRINT THE LETTER OF THE CORRECT ANSWER IN THE SPACE AT THE RIGHT.*

1. Which one of the following is an INCORRECT safety guideline? 1.____

   A. All working conditions and equipment should be considered carefully before beginning an operation.
   B. Aisles should be lighted properly.
   C. Personnel should be provided with protective clothing essential to safe performance of a task.
   D. In manual lifting, the worker must keep his knees straight and lift with the arm muscles.

2. Of the following, the supply item with the GREATEST susceptibility to spontaneous heating is 2.____

   A. alcohol, ethyl   B. kerosene
   C. candles   D. turpentine

Questions 3-7.

DIRECTIONS: Questions 3 through 7 are descriptions of accidents that occurred in a warehouse. For each accident, choose the letter in front of the safety measure that is MOST likely to prevent a repetition of the accident indicated.

SAFETY MEASURE

   A. Posting warning signs
   B. Redesign of layout or facilities
   C. Repairing, improving or replacing supplies, tools or equipment
   D. Training the staff in safe practices

3. After a new all-glass door was installed at the entrance to the warehouse, one of the employees banged his head into the door causing a large lump on his forehead when he failed to realize that the door was closed. 3.____

4. While tieing up a package with manila rope, an employee got several small rope splinters in his right hand and he had to have medical treatment to remove the splinters. 4.____

5. An employee discovered a small fire in a wastepaper basket but was unable to prevent it from spreading because all the nearby fire extinguishers were inaccessible due to skids of material being stacked in front of the extinguishers. 5.____

6. When a laborer attempted to drop the tailgate of a delivery truck while the truck was being backed into the loading dock, he had his fingers crushed when the truck continued to move while he was working on lowering the tailgate. 6.____

109

7. An employee carrying a carton with both hands tripped over a broom which had been left lying in an aisle by another employee after the latter had swept the aisle.

7._____

8. Safety experts agree that accidents can probably BEST be prevented by

    A. developing safety consciousness among employees
    B. developing a program which publicizes major accidents
    C. penalizing employees the first time they do not follow safety procedures
    D. giving recognition to employees with accident-free records

8._____

9. The accident records of many agencies indicate that most on-the-job injuries are caused by the unsafe acts of their employees.
Which one of the following statements pinpoints the MOST probable cause of this safety problem?

    A. Responsibility for preventing on-the-job accidents has not been delegated.
    B. Lack of proper supervision has permitted these unsafe actions to continue.
    C. No consideration has been given to eliminating environmental job hazards.
    D. Penalties for causing on-the-job accidents are not sufficiently severe.

9._____

10. Which of the following methods is LEAST essential to the success of an accident prevention program?

    A. Determining corrective measures by analyzing the causes of accidents and making recommendations to eliminate them
    B. Educating employees as to the importance of safe working conditions and methods
    C. Determining accident causes by seeking out the conditions from which each accident has developed
    D. Holding each supervisor responsible for accidents occurring during the on-the-job performance of his immediate subordinates

10._____

11. The effectiveness of a public relations program in a public agency is BEST indicated by the

    A. amount of mass media publicity favorable to the policies of the agency
    B. morale of those employees who directly serve the patrons of the agency
    C. public's understanding and support of the agency's program and policies
    D. number of complaints received by the agency from patrons using its facilities

11._____

12. Buttered bread and coffee dropped on an office floor in a terminal are

    A. minor hazards which should cause no serious injury
    B. unattractive, but not dangerous
    C. the most dangerous types of office hazards
    D. hazards which should be corrected immediately

12._____

13. A laborer was sent upstairs to get a 20-pound sack of rock salt. While going downstairs and reading the printing on the sack, he fell, and the sack of rock salt fell and broke his toe.
Which of the following is MOST likely to have been the MOST important cause of the accident?
The

13._____

- A. stairs were beginning to become worn
- B. laborer was carrying too heavy a sack of rock salt
- C. rock salt was in a place that was too inaccessible
- D. laborer was not careful about the way he went down the stairs

14. A COMMONLY recommended safe distance between the foot of an extension ladder and the wall against which it is placed is

- A. 3 feet for ladders less than 18 feet in height
- B. between 3 feet and 6 feet for ladders less than 18 feet in length
- C. 1/8 the length of the extended ladder
- D. 1/4 the length of the extended ladder

15. The BEST type of fire extinguisher for electrical fires is the _____ extinguisher.

- A. dry chemical
- B. foam
- C. carbon monoxide
- D. baking soda-acid

16. A Class A extinguisher should be used for fires in

- A. potassium, magnesium, zinc, sodium
- B. electrical wiring
- C. oil, gasoline
- D. wood, paper, and textiles

17. The one of the following which is NOT a safe practice when lifting heavy objects is:

- A. Keep the back as nearly upright as possible
- B. If the object feels too heavy, keep lifting until you get help
- C. Spread the feet apart
- D. Use the arm and leg muscles

18. In a shop, it would be MOST necessary to provide a fitted cover on the metal container for

- A. old paint brushes
- B. oily rags and waste
- C. sand
- D. broken glass

19. Safety shoes usually have the unique feature of

- A. extra hard heels and soles to prevent nails from piercing the shoes
- B. special leather to prevent the piercing of the shoes by falling objects
- C. a metal guard over the toes which is built into the shoes
- D. a non-slip tread on the heels and soles

20. Of the following, the MOST important factor contributing to a helper's safety on the job is for him to

- A. work slowly
- B. wear gloves
- C. be alert
- D. know his job well

21. If it is necessary for you to lift one end of a piece of heavy equipment with a crowbar in order to allow a maintainer to work underneath it, the BEST of the following procedures to follow is to

    A. support the handle of the bar on a box
    B. insert temporary blocks to support the piece
    C. call the supervisor to help you
    D. wear heavy gloves

22. Of the following, the MOST important reason for not letting oily rags accumulate in an open storage bin is that they

    A. may start a fire by spontaneous combustion
    B. will drip oil onto other items in the bin
    C. may cause a foul odor
    D. will make the area messy

23. Of the following, the BEST method to employ in putting out a gasoline fire is to

    A. use a bucket of water
    B. smother it with rags
    C. use a carbon dioxide extinguisher
    D. use a carbon tetrachloride extinguisher

24. When opening an emergency exit door set in the sidewalk, the door should be raised slowly to avoid

    A. a sudden rush of air from the street
    B. making unnecessary noise
    C. damage to the sidewalk
    D. injuring pedestrians

25. The BEST reason to turn off lights when cleaning lampshades on electrical fixtures is to

    A. conserve energy
    B. avoid electrical shock
    C. prevent breakage of lightbulbs
    D. prevent unnecessary eye strain

KEY (CORRECT ANSWERS)

1. D
2. D
3. A
4. D
5. B

6. D
7. D
8. A
9. B
10. D

11. C
12. D
13. D
14. D
15. A

16. D
17. B
18. B
19. C
20. C

21. B
22. A
23. C
24. D
25. B

TEST 2

DIRECTIONS: Each question or incomplete statement is followed by several suggested answers or completions. Select the one that BEST answers the question or completes the statement. *PRINT THE LETTER OF THE CORRECT ANSWER IN THE SPACE AT THE RIGHT.*

1. The MOST important reason for roping off a work area in a terminal is to

    A. protect the public
    B. protect the repair crew
    C. prevent distraction of the crew by the public
    D. prevent delays to the public

    1.____

2. Shoes which have a sponge rubber sole should NOT be worn around a work area because such a sole

    A. will wear quickly
    B. is not waterproof
    C. does not keep the feet warm
    D. is easily punctured by steel objects

    2.____

3. When repair work is being done on an elevated structure, canvas spreads are suspended under the working area MAINLY to

    A. reduce noise   B. discourage crowds
    C. protect the structure   D. protect pedestrians

    3.____

4. It is poor practice to hold a piece of wood in the hands or lap when tightening a screw in the wood.
   This is for the reason that

    A. sufficient leverage cannot be obtained
    B. the screwdriver may bend
    C. the wood will probably split
    D. personal injury is likely to result

    4.____

5. Steel helmets give workers the MOST protection from

    A. falling objects   B. eye injuries
    C. fire   D. electric shock

    5.____

6. It is POOR practice to wear goggles

    A. when chipping stone
    B. when using a grinder
    C. while climbing or descending ladders
    D. when handling molten metal

    6.____

7. When using a brace and bit to bore a hole completely through a partition, it is MOST important to

    7.____

A. lean heavily on the brace and bit
B. maintain a steady turning speed all through the job
C. have the body in a position that will not be easily thrown off balance
D. reverse the direction of the bit at frequent intervals

8. Gloves should be used when handling   8.____

   A. lanterns   B. wooden rules
   C. heavy ropes   D. all small tools

Questions 9-16.

DIRECTIONS: Questions 9 through 16, inclusive, are based on the ladder safety rules given below. Read these rules fully before answering these items.

LADDER SAFETY RULES

When a ladder is placed on a slightly uneven supporting surface, use a flat piece of board or small wedge to even up the ladder feet. To secure the proper angle for resting a ladder, it should be placed so that the distance from the base of the ladder to the supporting wall is 1/4 the length of the ladder. To avoid overloading a ladder, only one person should work on a ladder at a time. Do not place a ladder in front of a door. When the top rung of a ladder rests against a pole, the ladder should be lashed securely. Clear loose stones or debris from the ground around the base of a ladder before climbing. While on a ladder, do not attempt to lean so that any part of the body, except arms or hands, extends more than 12 inches beyond the side rail. Always face the ladder when ascending or descending. When carrying ladders through buildings, watch for ceiling globes and lighting fixtures. Avoid the use of rolling ladders as scaffold supports.

9. A small wedge is used to   9.____

   A. even up the feet of a ladder resting on an uneven surface
   B. lock the wheels of a roller ladder
   C. secure the proper resting angle for a ladder
   D. secure a ladder against a pole

10. An 8 foot ladder resting against a wall should be so inclined that the distance between the base of the ladder and the wall is _____ feet.   10.____

    A. 2   B. 5   C. 7   D. 9

11. A ladder should be lashed securely when   11.____

    A. it is placed in front of a door
    B. loose stones are on the ground near the base of the ladder
    C. the top rung rests against a pole
    D. two people are working from the same ladder

12. Rolling ladders   12.____

    A. should be used for scaffold supports
    B. should not be used for scaffold supports
    C. are useful on uneven ground
    D. should be used against a pole

13. When carrying a ladder through a building, it is necessary to

   A. have two men to carry it
   B. carry the ladder vertically
   C. watch for ceiling globes
   D. face the ladder while carrying it

14. It is POOR practice to

   A. lash a ladder securely at any time
   B. clear debris from the base of a ladder before climbing
   C. even up the feet of a ladder resting on slightly uneven ground
   D. place a ladder in front of a door

15. A person on a ladder should NOT extend his head beyond the side rail by more than _____ inches.

   A. 12   B. 9   C. 7   D. 5

16. The MOST important reason for permitting only one person to work on a ladder at a time is that

   A. both could not face the ladder at one time
   B. the ladder will be overloaded
   C. time would be lost going up and down the ladder
   D. they would obstruct each other

17. Many portable electric power tools, such as electric drills, have a third conductor in the power lead which is used to connect the case of the tool to a grounded part of the electric outlet.
   The reason for this extra conductor is to

   A. have a spare wire in case one power wire should break
   B. strengthen the power lead so it cannot easily be damaged
   C. prevent the user of the tool from being shocked
   D. enable the tool to be used for long periods of time without overheating

18. Protective goggles should NOT be worn when

   A. standing on a ladder drilling a steel beam
   B. descending a ladder after completing a job
   C. chipping concrete near a third rail
   D. sharpening a cold chisel on a grinding stone

19. When the foot of an extension ladder, placed against a high wall, rests on a sidewalk or another such similar surface, it is advisable to tie a rope between the bottom rung of the ladder and a point on the wall opposite this rung.
   This is done to prevent

   A. people from walking under the ladder
   B. another worker from removing the ladder
   C. the ladder from vibrating when ascending or descending
   D. the foot of the ladder from slipping

20. In construction work, practically all accidents can be blamed on the

    A. failure of an individual to give close attention to the job assigned to him
    B. use of improper tools
    C. lack of cooperation among the men in a gang
    D. fact that an incompetent man was placed in a key position

21. If it is necessary for you to do some work with your hands under a piece of heavy equipment while a fellow worker lifts up and holds one end of it by means of a pinch bar, one important precaution you should take is to

    A. wear gloves
    B. watch the bar to be ready if it slips
    C. insert a temporary block to support the piece
    D. work as fast as possible

22. Employees of the transit system whose work requires them to enter upon the tracks in the subway are cautioned not to wear loose fitting clothing.
    The MOST important reason for this caution is that loose fitting clothing may

    A. interfere when men are using heavy tools
    B. catch on some projection of a passing train
    C. tear more easily than snug fitting clothing
    D. give insufficient protection against subway dust

23. The MOST important reason for insisting on neatness in maintenance quarters is that it

    A. keeps the men busy in slack periods
    B. prevents tools from becoming rusty
    C. makes a good impression on visitors and officials
    D. decreases the chances of accidents to employees

24. Maintenance workers whose duties require them to do certain types of work generally work in pairs.
    The LEAST likely of the following possible reasons for this practice is that

    A. some of the work requires two men
    B. the men can help each other in case of accident
    C. there is too much equipment for one man to carry
    D. it protects against vandalism

25. A foreman reprimands a helper for actions in violation of the rules and regulations.
    The BEST reaction of the helper in this situation is to

    A. tell the foreman that he was careful and that he did not take any chances
    B. explain that he took this action to save time
    C. keep quiet and accept the criticism
    D. demand that the foreman show him the rule he violated

KEY (CORRECT ANSWERS)

1. A
2. D
3. D
4. D
5. A

6. C
7. C
8. C
9. A
10. A

11. C
12. B
13. C
14. D
15. A

16. B
17. C
18. B
19. D
20. A

21. C
22. B
23. D
24. D
25. C
